PRAISE

MONEY: GOD OR GIFT

"One of the best books on money I've read."

–Matt Chandler, president of the Acts 29 Network, author, and pastor of The Village Church (thevillagechurch.net)

"At the end of the day, every Christian is a steward and not an owner. Jamie teaches us how to steward well the resources that God has given us."

–Lecrae, Grammy Award-winning musical artist (lecrae.com)

"If you are looking for a good, solid book on money—one that provides a biblical overview and practical application—this is it."

–Michael Hyatt, best-selling author, public speaker, and renowned blogger (michaelhyatt.com)

"As a 23-year-old kid, I came into the NFL with no financial literacy. I needed to biblically understand God's intentions for my finances. Not only does Jamie clearly articulate a biblical view of money, he also beautifully integrates the blanket of grace that Christ uses to continuously covers us while we learn and live out authentic financial freedom."

–Garrett Gilkey, offensive guard, Tampa Bay Buccaneers

"Jesus talked about money more than he did about heaven and hell combined. Jamie Munson helps us understand the text of Scripture and the heart of Jesus with regard to money."

–Darrin Patrick, vice president of the Acts 29 Network, author, and pastor of The Journey (thejourney.org)

"The very first thing I did after reading Money: God or Gift was order a copy for every single person in my church. It was that good. This book is practical, inspiring, and above all, gospel-saturated."

–Noel Heikkinen, pastor of Riverview Church (rivchurch.com)

"Here it is: An accessible, clear, grace-filled book on money, firmly grounded in Scripture. Jamie's book is a gift to Jesus' Church."

–Elliot Grudem, lead pastor for church planting, Vintage Church (vintagenc.com)

BULK ORDERS

MORE *MONEY* FOR LESS

Want to read *Money: God or Gift* with your church or small group? Discount prices available on bulk orders.

Visit theMoneyMission.com for details.

MONEY:
GOD OR GIFT

JAMIE MUNSON

theMoneyMission.com

ISBN: 978-0988754348

TABLE OF CONTENTS

APPENDIX

FOREWORD

by Darrin Patrick

Money. Few words evoke more emotion than this simple word.

Money triggers our dreams. It can get us on TV. It can get us into a new social circle. If we have enough, it can even get us an audience with the president! But money also taps into our nightmares. Can we afford this new baby? Can we pay for the cost of this operation? Is my job secure? Few things expose the soul of human beings like the making and using of money. It is that powerful.

Money reveals what we worship, that which our hearts trust. Jesus said, "Where your treasure is, there your heart will be also" (Matt. 6:21). In other words, if you want to know what you treasure, look at your bank account. The way we use money reveals not only what is important to us, but also our very identity—what we use to feel personally significant, socially connected, and emotionally secure. We may not worship money, but we do worship with our money.

Some of us are spenders. It is so effortless. Whether it is clothes, gadgets, or toys for the kids, we find something to blow our money on. We still haven't figured out if the money is burning holes in our pockets or just flying out of our wallets. We struggle to save. Giving is impossible. We are out of control, and we know it.

A few of us are good at saving and investing. We're able to fight our impulses and look to the future. This is part of what it means to be a good steward, which you will become if you follow Jaime's advice. But if money has become our primary security, we cross over into idolatry: trusting our money instead of our God. We may be in control, but we are full of anxiety as well.

Andrew Carnegie, one of the richest men in his day, understood the power of money. At the age of 33, he resolved to take no more than $50,000 per year, giving the surplus of his earning for "benevolent purposes." On New Year's Eve in 1868, he explained this decision:

> The amassing of wealth is one of the worst species of idolatry—no idol is more debasing than the worship of money. . . . To continue much longer overwhelmed by business cares and with most of my thoughts wholly upon the way to make more money in the shortest time, must degrade me beyond hope of permanent recovery.[1]

His journal entry was filled with punctuation, syntax, and spelling errors. Carnegie grew up illiterate. Yet in harnessing the power of money, stewarding it well rather than being ruled by it, he helped millions become literate through the thousands of libraries he funded.

Money: God or Gift is for spenders, savers, and everyone in between. It is by far one of the most practical and thoughtful books on money I have ever read. Read and heed these words. Use the power of money for the good of your own soul and the good of the world.

---

1. Andrew Carnegie, *The Autobiography of Andrew Carnegie*, ed. John C. Van Dyke (London: Constable & Co. Ltd., 1920), note 30, http://www.gutenberg.org/files/17976/17976-h/17976-h.htm#FNanchor_30_30.

INTRODUCTION
"THE LAST TABOO"

This is a book about your money and God.

If you're like a lot of people, both of these topics make you rather uncomfortable.[2] In 2014, Reuters called money "the last taboo."[3] I agree. Our personal finances reveal a lot about who we are and what we care about, and I don't enjoy sharing that level of vulnerability on a casual basis. Whether rich, poor, or somewhere in between, it's all too easy to cast judgment on people based on what we know about their money. Not to mention the fact that money can rip up a relationship like a cancelled check through envy, greed, pride, and selfish ambition.

No wonder we avoid the subject.

TOO BIG TO IGNORE

Like most difficult topics, however, we avoid important conversations to our own detriment. Delay makes the

---

2. Michelle Crouch, "Poll: Card debt the No. 1 taboo subject," CreditCards.com, April 15, 2013, http://www.creditcards.com/credit-card-news/poll-credit-card-taboo-subject-2013-1276.php.

3. Chris Taylor, "The Last Taboo: Why nobody talks about money," Reuters, March 27, 2014, http://www.reuters.com/article/2014/03/27/us-money-conversation-idUSBREA2Q1UN20140327.

inevitable all the more painful. My hope is that within the privacy of these pages you'll grant me the honor of helping you think through finance, faith, and your future.

If you're reading this book as part of a group, I encourage you to take a risk and make the most of it. Open up. Go there. Allow yourself to be stretched, challenged, and changed. The book is my effort to summarize what I've learned about money as I've grown from debt-stricken teenager to the primary provider for my family of six. These principles transformed my life in many ways practical and profound, and I wrote everything down so that other people might experience the same.

A HISTORY OF *MONEY: GOD OR GIFT*

I want to help, which is why I served as a pastor for many years. The first edition of this book was written during that time. In 2010, our church was studying the book of Luke, specifically Luke chapter 12.

We gave a free copy of *Money* to everyone in the congregation in order to encourage people to learn about what God has to say on the subject. Many other churches picked up the book as well, and provided very gracious responses. In order to continue to make this resource available, I decided to publish the book again in a new-and-improved format.

The revised and expanded edition of *Money* contains almost all of the content from the first time around, along with some new material. I restructured the big ideas to make the book more accessible and readable, since the audience now extends beyond a specific church studying a specific set of verses. The new small group discussion guide in the back of the book provides a helpful roadmap for churches, ministries, and families who'd like to study this topic together.

DON'T BELIEVE IN GOD?

For any folks out there with an aversion to Bible references and God talk, I invite you to keep reading anyway. I've kept the book short on purpose, so worst-case scenario you lose an hour or two.

Best-case scenario, maybe you pick up a few helpful ideas, strategies, or even a whole new perspective on life and money. A few hours is a low-risk investment with the possibility of less stress and more joy in return. If you already have your finances dialed in, great. Maybe you'll pick up a tidbit here and there. But if you're in any way dissatisfied with your money, give this book a try. You may not learn how to become a millionaire, but you might be surprised by a different take on personal finance.

Christians and non-Christians, rich and poor, blue-collar and white-collar, retired, full-time, and unemployed—this book has a little something for everyone. Even if you're not ready to talk about money, I'm glad you're willing to read about it, and I hope *Money* serves you well.

CHAPTER ONE
HATE IT

"No one can serve two masters, for either he will hate the one and love the other, or he will be devoted to the one and despise the other. You cannot serve God and money."
—*Jesus* [4]

What are you afraid of?

The best place to start a book about money is not with budgets and balance sheets, economics and financial theory, or debt management and career development.

The best place to begin is our fears.

That's exactly what Jesus does in Luke chapter 12. Before launching into a brilliant teaching about money, wealth, and possessions, he begins with these stern yet comforting words:

I tell you, my friends, do not fear those who kill the body, and after that have nothing more that they can do. But I will warn you whom to fear: fear him who, after he has killed, has authority to cast into hell. Yes, I tell you, fear him! Are not five sparrows sold for two pennies? And not one of them is forgotten before God.

4. Matt. 6:24.

Why, even the hairs of your head are all numbered. Fear not; you are of more value than many sparrows.[5]

The Bible connects fear and love and worship in a way that can sound confusing. "Perfect love casts out fear," the Apostle John tells us[6] after Proverbs has already said, "The fear of the LORD is the beginning of knowledge; fools despise wisdom and instruction."[7]

Clearly, Jesus embraces the love/fear paradox when he reminds us that the only one who can wreck us for eternity is also the only one who loves us right down to every hair on our heads. Yes, a level of raw, gut-wrenching fright is probably to be expected when it comes to an encounter with God the infinite Creator of the universe, and we certainly see this response throughout Scripture.[8] But fear in the biblical sense goes much deeper than terror, and it's much more complex than the sort of intimidation wielded by tyrants, bullies, and other lesser gods that use fear as a weapon. What you choose to fear will control you.

BAD FEAR

"Fear and worry reveal us," writes theologian and psychologist Dr. Ed Welch. "They reveal the things that we love and value."[9] In turn, the things that we love and value are

---

5. Luke 12:4–7.

6. 1 John 4:18.

7. Prov. 1:7.

8. Ex. 20:18; Isa. 6:5; Rev. 1:17.

9. Edward T. Welch, *Running Scared* (Greensboro, NC: New Growth Press, 2007), 13.

the things that we worship. For example, children, money, and friendships become idols when we fear death, insecurity, and rejection. Our happiness then gets tied up in the well-being of our kids, the size of our bank balance, or the health of our relationships—all of which will eventually falter and fail.

Everybody is afraid—afraid of suffering, loss, rejection, failure, embarrassment—because everybody cares about something, even if it's just themselves. And so we pour out our resources, our energy, and our days in an attempt to protect what we love from whatever threatens it. The effort is in vain, however, because children die. People lose their jobs. Families disintegrate. Houses burn down. Friends move away. Stock markets crash.

We waste life by worrying about things we can't control and fearing things we can't avoid. The Bible calls this "striving after wind."[10] In the end, it is folly—the opposite of wisdom.

GOOD FEAR

Fear is unavoidable, which means what we fear is of great importance. The fear of the Lord is not a caution against an abusive father with cosmic mood swings and unpredictable behavior. Fear of the Lord leads us to worship him: acknowledging with reverence and awe that God is the all-knowing, all-powerful, ever-present, always-good Creator and Sustainer of everyone and everything.

The fear of the Lord is the only thing that can prevent us from succumbing to all of the other fears that

---

10. Eccl. 2:17.

steal our lives away. Despite our best efforts, ultimately we can't control anything. God, however, can control everything. We can trust him because he is infinite, eternal, and unchangeable in his being, wisdom, power, holiness, justice, goodness, and truth.[11] As John Newton wrote in "Amazing Grace": *'Twas grace that taught my heart to fear, and grace my fears relieved.*

The fear of the Lord is wisdom because only God deserves our worship. To live otherwise is folly.

MONEY + FEAR = WORRY

When it comes to money, fear usually emerges in the form of worry. Financial anxiety is fear that eclipses all reverence for God. Worry reveals our lack of faith in his promises. To put it plainly, worry is sin. Dr. Ed Welch explains this well:

> Worry, therefore, is not simply an emotion that erodes our quality of life or a pain to be alleviated. It is a misdirected love that should be confessed. It is trying to manage our world apart from God. It is making life about our needs, desires, and wants . . . [F]ind anxiety about finances and you find sin; it is as simple as that.[12]

God redeems our worry by using it as a flashing neon arrow that points right to our sin. His objective is not to make us feel bad by illuminating our shortcomings,

---

11. Westminster Shorter Catechism, Q.4.

12. Welch, *Running Scared*, 163.

but to reveal our desperate need for a better, more powerful, more loving God: Jesus. If we see worry as an emotion or as pain, we can only mitigate or manage it. This makes us slaves to anxiety, mastered by the thing that we fear. But when we understand worry as sin, however, it is dealt with at the cross. Through Jesus' death we are forgiven and set free from all sin—including worry.

LOVE IT OR HATE IT

Over the course of this book, we'll address many common fears, worries, errors, and sin related to money, but Jesus sums up the big idea in one verse: "No one can serve two masters, for either he will hate the one and love the other, or he will be devoted to the one and despise the other. You cannot serve God and money."[13]

One of the most commonly misquoted verses in the entire Bible is 1 Timothy 6:10. Contrary to what you may have heard, it does not label money as the root of all evil. Rather, "the *love of money* is a root of all kinds of evils" (emphasis added). People die for it. Kill for it. Give their lives in pursuit of it. But it's not money's fault. People love money because it represents security, comfort, deliverance, and status. All bogus, of course, because God is the only master who can make good on those promises.

Hate is a strong word, to be sure, but I hope it sticks in your mind as you continue to read. Let's be clear: Jesus does not call us to hate money itself, but to hate money as our master. Don't desire it, pine for it, live

---

13. Matt. 6:24.

for it. Money is not evil, but when we let it rule our lives money provokes fear, worry, greed, pride and other brands of evil in our hearts. Therefore, we must approach the subject wisely and carefully in order to keep money in its rightful place. The philosopher-scientist Francis Bacon gets credit for saying, "Money makes a good servant, but a bad master." When received and used properly, money is an excellent, useful, helpful gift from God, a tool for worshiping Jesus and honoring the Lord. My great hope and prayer is to help you wield this tool well. Without hating money as master, however, we're likely to fear, worship, and love it rather than God.

To fear the money god is slavery. There's never enough and it offers no salvation. To fear the Lord is wisdom and freedom. When an unexpected bill shows up in the mail, when the car breaks down, when a major business decision looms, or when foreclosure seems imminent, we are free to "fear not,"[14] knowing that our future, our eternity, and our lives are in the stable, trustworthy care of his hand: "Keep your life free from love of money, and be content with what you have, for he has said, 'I will never leave you nor forsake you.' So we can confidently say, 'The Lord is my helper; I will not fear.'"[15]

If our hearts belong to Jesus and our lives are devoted to his mission, we need not avoid, demonize, or fear money. We can love God, love people, and use money to enjoy life and serve him.

---

14. Luke 12:7.

15. Heb. 13:5–6.

CHAPTER TWO
STEWARD IT

"But who am I, and what is my people, that we should be
able thus to offer willingly? For all things come from
you, and of your own have we given you."
—King David [16]

Everything we have comes from God and belongs to God:
life, family, money, resources, time, job, talents . . . *every-*
thing.[17] We are stewards. All things belong to God, and he
gives to us according to his grace and goodness.

Many Christians nod their heads in agreement,
but for the most part we walk around like we own the
place. Rather than cultivating humble appreciation, we
covet a higher standard of living. Rather than gratitude for
his grace, we exhibit greed for our own gain. The difference between these two outlooks influences and directs
every aspect of life (see table, next page):

---

16. 1 Chron. 29:14.

17. John 3:27; 1 Cor. 4:7.

	Gratitude	Greed
Attitude	Humility (Phil. 2:3)	Grumbling (Phil. 2:15)
Perspective	Grace: "I am a sinner who deserves death but Jesus paid the price and gave me his perfect righteousness."	Entitlement: "I am a good person who deserves heaven—plus a comfortable, pain-free existence in the meantime."
Desire	Jesus is enough to satisfy my life.	Jesus is not enough. I want wealth/fame/comfort/power as well.
Money	God gives. Therefore my money is his, and I use it to glorify him.	I earn. Therefore my money is mine, and I use it however I please.
Possessions	Contentment: I have enough.	Covetous: I never have enough.
Church	Serve as a member of God's family	Be served as a consumer
Job	Work heartily for the Lord, cultivating thanks for God's provision (Deut. 8:17; Col. 3:23).	Work begrudgingly for the man; becoming bitter and jealous against others (James 3:16).
Family	A blessing to embrace	A burden to escape
Future	Eternal: optimistic/hopeful (2 Cor. 4:7–9)	Temporal: pessimistic/anxious
Worship	Time, energy, and resources go to God.	Time, energy, and resources go to me.
Identity	Jesus and his achievement	My abilities and my achievements
Giving	Generous	Guilt- or gain-motivated (or non-existent)
Body	His temple, bought with a price	My property, I'll do what I want
Life	His, lived for his glory	Mine, lived for my glory

Either everything on the list is his, given to me for a

purpose, or it's mine, and I'm entitled to it because . . . pick your justification: I'm a good person, I work hard, I'm intelligent, I earned it, karma, and so on. A perspective of stewardship marks the difference between a life of gratitude and a life of greed. Recognize destructive greed in your own life by listening for the grumble. Maybe you can hear it when the church takes up a collection, or when you get overlooked for a promotion at work, or when your best friend rolls up in a brand new car. Ongoing discontentment, entitlement, anger, resentment, and bitterness cloud conversation and douse any joy.

We're all susceptible to this mentality that puts us at odds with our humble position as stewards. "It begins with a grumbling mood," says C.S. Lewis, "and yourself still distinct from it: perhaps criticizing it. And yourself, in a dark hour, may will that mood, embrace it. Ye can repent and come out of it again. But there may come a day when you can do that no longer."[18] We can choose to grumble or, with God's help, guidance, and grace, we can choose to be grateful.[19] Little by little, our choice of mood sets the course for a day, which becomes a week, which becomes a year, which becomes the theme of our lifetime.

That said, the Bible does connect physical work with material reward, obedience with blessing. But life does not always follow the formula, and "the same event happens to the righteous and the wicked, to the good and the evil."[20] Outside of the fact that the world is cursed

18. C.S. Lewis, *The Great Divorce* (New York: HarperCollins, 2001), 77–78.

19. Col. 3:15.

20. Eccl. 9:2.

with sin, we cannot explain exactly why bad things happen to good people, or why some bad guys enjoy the good life. We do know, however, that God's economy is not measured by dollars and cents adding up in tidy equations, but by righteousness and justice that play out over the course of eternity. In this system, the "have nots" may not be so poor after all, and the "haves" best not get too comfortable.

IT'S NOT ABOUT THE MONEY . . .

God's grace is a cosmic reality with enormous implications. Jesus offers "eternal life"[21] and "treasures in heaven, where neither moth nor rust destroys and where thieves do not break in and steal."[22] In the meantime, we enjoy more than we deserve on earth. In short, we're all "haves" in Jesus. Even if our sole possession is the air left in our lungs, that's still an occasion to praise him with our last breath because "to live is Christ and to die is gain."[23]

The prosperity theology common in many Christian traditions confuses the matter by associating material riches in this life with God's blessing and favor. Are you wealthy? Congratulations, God is pleased with you! Are you poor? For shame, oh ye of little faith.

The Bible consistently teaches a more beautiful truth that dismantles prosperity theology: God's blessing is not for sale, and his grace is free.[24] If anything, Jesus

21. John 5:24.

22. Matt. 6:20.

23. Phil. 1:21.

24. Among many examples, see Isa. 55:1; Rom. 6:23; Rev. 22:17.

promises a great reversal of fortune to come, when the "have nots" become "haves," and vice versa. In the book of Revelation, for example, he provides a stern rebuke for the early Christian church in Laodicea, a wealthy congregation characterized by their "lukewarm" faith: "For you say, 'I am rich. I have prospered, and I need nothing,' not realizing that you are wretched, pitiable, poor, blind, and naked."[25] Likewise, we may prosper financially and "need nothing," but without Jesus and his work in our hearts, we don't actually have anything.

We shouldn't minimize the Bible's warnings to the rich, but poverty theology takes this perspective to another extreme. While prosperity theology links personal holiness to personal wealth, poverty theology makes the opposite error by teaching that it is godly to be poor and sinful to be rich. There are many problems with this perspective, starting with the fact that Jesus was rich before coming to earth,[26] and he will be rich as the forever king reigning over a perfectly sinless kingdom.

The Apostle Paul addresses the allure of poverty theology when he writes about our tendency to invent religious restrictions beyond the Bible: "These have indeed an appearance of wisdom in promoting self-made religion and asceticism and severity to the body, but they are of no value in stopping the indulgence of the flesh."[27]

Money does not indicate one's position before God, because God doesn't look at the bank account; he

---

25. Rev. 3:17.

26. 2 Cor. 8:9.

27. Col. 2:23.

looks at the heart. [28] In this regard, the "haves" are no better (prosperity theology) or worse (poverty theology) than the "have nots." The life of Paul illustrates this well. He "learned the secret of being content in any and every situation, whether well fed or hungry, whether living in plenty or in want." [29] God does not require his people to be poor, nor does he promise that all of his disciples will be wealthy. As Paul teaches so well, our righteousness, our salvation, our acceptance before God, our faith, our blessing have nothing to do with money and everything to do with Jesus. [30]

. . . BUT THE MONEY STILL MATTERS

Just because it's all about Jesus doesn't mean that money doesn't matter. In fact, New Testament scholar Craig Blomberg calls stewardship of material possessions "the most important test-case of one's profession of discipleship," [31] and names materialism as "the single biggest competitor with authentic Christianity for the hearts and souls of millions in our world today." [32]

What we do with our money—how we steward God's money—nudges our life toward him or away from him, "for where your treasure is, there your heart will be also." [33] Every financial transaction reveals our heart by

28. 1 Sam. 16:7; Jer. 17:10.

29. Phil. 4:12.

30. 2 Cor. 1:20.

31. Craig L. Blomberg, *Neither Poverty nor Riches* (Downers Grove, IL: InterVarsity Press, 2000), 127.

32. Ibid., 132.

33. Matt. 6:21.

presenting an opportunity to worship Jesus and serve his kingdom, or worship ourselves and serve our own lesser kingdom. All of us, "haves" and "have nots" alike, will use our money to serve the priorities of the god we worship.

One woman's story illustrates this principle beautifully. She was a poor woman, certainly a "have not" by our common monetary standard. She ducked into church one day to slip a couple coins into the collection. Her contribution would have gone totally unnoticed, perhaps even uncounted and dismissed as a negligible amount hardly worth the bother, if not for one person sitting nearby. Jesus had been watching the box, and heard the heavy clatter of many coins as the rich took turns dumping small fortunes into the box. It wasn't until the woman "put in two small copper coins" that Jesus spoke up and said, "Truly, I tell you, this poor widow has put in more than all of them. For they all contributed out of their abundance, but she out of her poverty put in all she had to live on." [34]

FOR RICH AND POOR ALIKE

God doesn't care how much you have, but he does care how you use it. Since stewardship is a gesture of the heart, the amount of money involved doesn't matter. The categories of rich and poor, prosperity and poverty, or have and have-not, are less important than the categories of righteous and unrighteous. [35] The righteous rich and righteous

34. Luke 21:1–4.

35. Mark Driscoll and Gerry Breshears, *Doctrine: What Christians Should Believe* (Wheaton, IL: Crossway, 2010), 389–390.

poor work hard, give generously, and steward wisely. The number of zeroes involved may vary greatly, but God is equally pleased with the result, as we learn from the widow's sacrifice. On the other hand, the unrighteous rich and unrighteous poor steal, lie, and destroy for financial gain. The only difference is some move the bottom line better than others.

The wisdom of God's commands apply to rich and poor alike. The Bible does often challenge the rich directly and advocate for the poor specifically, because God loves the rich and does not want to see them enslaved to their money, and God loves the poor and wants to comfort them. But rather than prescribing a lot of directives—how much to give, where to invest, and when to retire—God simply provides principles that help us live in such a way that honors him, protects us, and allows us great freedom to live within the all-encompassing framework of his wisdom.

Money is a prop on the stage of God's story, used or pursued for good or for ill, to God's glory or to our own destruction. Through stewardship, we can avoid the traps of prosperity theology and poverty theology, cultivate a heart of gratitude for the gifts God has given, and use those gifts in a righteous manner to reflect the heart and priorities of Jesus.

For the remainder of this book, we'll look at a few specific ways to steward money, and what it looks like to budget, earn, spend, save, invest, give, and multiply money to the glory of God.

CHAPTER THREE
BUDGET IT

"The years of our life are seventy, or even by reason of strength eighty; yet their span is but toil and trouble; they are soon gone, and we fly away . . . So teach us to number our days that we may get a heart of wisdom."
—*Moses* [36]

Most people learn about money the hard way, if they ever learn about money at all. That was my story. My parents made decent money, especially by Montana standards, but they didn't know how to manage it.

One time we set off on a camping trip and decided to pick up some Aquasox along the way. We went to several stores before my folks forgot the shoes and decided to buy a 20-foot Bayliner instead. I was old enough to know the latest paycheck wouldn't cover the cost, and a brand new speedboat certainly wasn't in the budget, because we didn't have a budget. But I didn't know any different at the time. If impulse buying yielded water-skiing, then that sounded like a pretty sweet return on investment to me.

---

36. Ps. 90:10, 12.

5 APPROACHES TO BUDGETING

Of course, this way of thinking eventually led to some financial blunders of my own, which I'll share a bit later. Based on my family's mistakes and my own ill-advised decisions, along with a few scenarios I encountered in my years as a pastor, I've now identified at least four terrible budget strategies.

1. The Ignorance Is Bliss Plan
Check your balance at the ATM. If there's money in the account, score! Proceed to withdraw cash. No checkbook and no clue required.

2. The Parent Bailout Plan
When you run out of money, call your mom to inform her that you are broke once again. Wait for free money to arrive. This method may be cute when you're 7, but not when you're 27.

3. The Credit Card Plan
Conduct all of your purchasing on a credit card. When you reach the spending limit, obtain a new credit card. Repeat.

4. The Hand-to-Mouth Plan
Spend exactly what you earn and live paycheck-to-paycheck. You don't fall behind, but you also never get ahead.

Option #5 would be a real plan. Master money or it will master you. You don't have to be Warren Buffet, but good financial stewardship is impossible without a basic understanding and plan: a budget. Unlike the options above, a real plan honors God and can lead to great joy and relief.

BUDGET FOR JUDGMENT DAY

Jesus' lengthy sermon on money in Luke chapter 12 includes some dark turns. "Stay dressed for action," he says, before telling a couple stories about servants waiting for their master's return from a long journey.[37]

The "faithful and wise manager" will be blessed upon his master's return.[38] The manager who takes advantage of his master's absence will be cut to pieces.[39] The lazy manager and the ignorant manager both fail to prepare for difference reasons, but both will face a beating.[40] It doesn't get any nicer from there, as Jesus goes right into his fire and brimstone moment, proclaiming, "I came to cast fire on the earth, and would that it were already kindled!"[41]

If this strong language is unclear to you, suffice it to say that Jesus takes stewardship very seriously. He pulls no punches when he teaches about the day when each of us will answer for how we spent our time, how we used our money, and how we lived the life God gave us.

This is a heavy topic, and it may seem odd to leap from Judgment Day into a discussion about spreadsheets

---

37. Luke 12:35.

38. Luke 12:42–43.

39. Luke 12:47.

40. Luke 12:47–48.

41. Luke 12:49.

and budgets, but that's part of the problem. We minimize and compartmentalize certain aspects of life and choose to believe that God only cares about things like prayer, Bible reading, church attendance, and the token good deed from time to time. This is a lie we tell ourselves and a lie Satan is happy to perpetuate. The enemy wins when our money is distant from our walk with Jesus, because our hearts will remain equally distant as well,[42] and our resources will be less effective in the mission God has given us.

The unfaithful manager in Jesus' story falls prey to this mentality. The master is delayed, and, rather than cultivating a sense of anticipation, the manager begins to cut corners and justify his actions. What probably began as a small breach of decorum or minor compromise (*Surely my master won't miss one little sip of the good stuff*) quickly degenerates into the power trip from hell. It doesn't take long before the manager starts acting like he owns the place—chugging the wine, eating the food, and abusing the other servants.

We can't expect to be faithful with six figures if we don't know what to do with six dollars. That's the big idea of Jesus' story: "Everyone to whom much was given, of him much will be required."[43] As remedial or boring or unspiritual as it may sound to build a budget, planning is an essential component of faithful stewardship, financial wisdom, and glorifying God with your resources.

---

42. Matt. 6:21, again.

43. Luke 12:48.

PRAISE GOD WITH YOUR BUDGET

Singing and praying aren't the only ways we can respond to God's grace and goodness. We can glorify God with a life lived according to his Lordship, choosing to follow and honor him rather than running after the money god and tumbling headlong into financial slavery.

In other words, building a budget can be an act of worship. The process requires contemplation of all that God has given us, and prayerfully considering what he might be calling us to do with it.

God is not the only one who will benefit from your budget. Living with no plan and no budget is not freedom, it's a recipe for stress, hardship, and folly. The side effects of no financial planning are fear, anxiety, worry, depression, doubt, and even divorce. A 2012 study conducted at Texas Tech and Kansas State universities determined that "financial disagreements were the strongest disagreement types to predict divorce."[44] One researcher summarized, "Arguments about money is by far the top predictor of divorce. It's not children, sex, in-laws or anything else. It's money—for both men and women."[45]

Money without a budget is like a car without a dashboard. Imagine what it would be like to drive without

---

44. Jeffery Dew, Sonya Britt, and Sandra Huston, "Examining the Relationship Between Financial Issues and Divorce," Family Relations 61 (October 2012): 615–628, doi: 10.1111/j.1741-3729.2012.00715.x.

45. "Researcher finds correlation between financial arguments, decreased relationship satisfaction," Kansas State University, July 12, 2013, http://www.k-state.edu/media/newsreleases/jul13/predictingdivorce71113.html.

any dials, indicators, or panels whatsoever. You could probably manage for a little while, but try commuting dozens
of miles every day without ever knowing how fast you're
going, if the engine's about to explode, if the trunk is ajar,
or if you're about to run out of gas. Every outing becomes
a risky guessing game, and every safe trip merely delays the
inevitable crisis.

All guidelines, from a budget to the commands of
God, may feel restrictive. But the boundaries are there to
protect us and guide us. It's not the gas gauge's fault when
you sputter to a halt on the middle of the interstate. Our
own sin and poor decisions get us into trouble; wisdom
helps us stay out of it. And wisdom says make a plan, create
a budget, and obey God.

HOW TO MAKE A REAL PLAN

In the back of this book, I've included a worksheet to help
you get started on your budget. I also recommend Dave
Ramsey's *Total Money Makeover*, a very practical book
that includes lots of helpful tools for organizing personal
finances. In the meantime, however, here are six guiding
principles to keep in mind as you develop your budget.

1. Keep it simple.

Fancy software isn't necessary. Excel will do just fine, as will
a pencil and paper. If it helps to have some extra bells and
whistles, go for it. Otherwise, no need to overcomplicate.

2. Focus on priorities.

We'll hit this more in chapter 5, but the basic idea here is to decide where you want your money to go and why. Don't think in terms of wants and needs. Consider all of the places where your money could go, and then prioritize to ensure that the most important things get funded first.

3. Plan all of your expenses in advance.

Remove the emotional/impulse factor by deciding where your money is going before the time comes to spend it. Try to plan out your cash flow at least six months in advance.

4. Align your plans with reality.

Everyone has weekly, monthly, and annual expenses. Calculate your budget per year, and then determine what that looks like per month and per paycheck.

5. Be conservative.

Use extra cash for margin and try to live lean wherever you can. If you work in the service industry, consider living off your base salary so that you can save all of your tips. If you and your spouse both work, try to live off of one income. This will help you discipline your spending habits, save for emergencies or large purchases, and allow you to live generously.

6. Check your attitude.

Remember to cultivate an attitude of contentment rather than succumb to entitlement. Work hard, make the most of every opportunity, prepare for the rainy days, and roll with the punches.

Living with a plan doesn't mean you never deviate from the plan. On the contrary, the more prepared we are, the more likely we'll be ready to respond wisely and quickly to new opportunities. Prioritize and plan out the most important things: spend time with Jesus; budget; read the Bible; date your spouse; love your kids; get to know your neighbors; keep a calendar. Then when the time comes for spontaneity, you can enjoy it in good conscience rather than allowing it to derail the rest of your life.

Finally, all of this planning and preparation takes a lot of wisdom, so remember where wisdom comes from. Don't leave God out of your financial planning. Invite the Holy Spirit to guide you. He is our Helper, so ask him to help you, and follow where he leads. [46]

---

46. John 14:16.

CHAPTER FOUR
MAKE IT

Money is the answer for everything.
—King Solomon [47]

When my two daughters were ten and seven years old, they gave me a fifteen-slide PowerPoint presentation about how they wanted to upgrade their room, complete with a budget. A central part of their funding plan was a lemonade stand business called the Sweet and Sour Sisters. It was Sesame Street meets Shark Tank, and I responded to the concept with my whole-hearted, proud papa approval. The Sweet and Sour Sisters were in business, and to no one's surprise, they sold out in an hour.

My girls wanted to make some money, and here's what I did not tell them:

- Forget about the lemonade stand. I'll pay for your room.
- God's grace is free, so why isn't your lemonade? Don't be so greedy.
- Are you sure you're passionate about lemonade? Why don't you find work that's more fulfilling?

Making money is a good thing. Money provides a means, though of course not the only means, to

---

47. Eccl. 10:19, NIV.

accomplish goals, solve problems, put food on the table, open doors, care for the needy, develop community, and fulfill little dreams (purchase pre-teen bedroom decor) or big dreams (start a business, travel the world).

Money is such a useful, powerful tool, it's no wonder people will do just about anything to get more of it. By no means do I advocate a life of unbridled acquisition, but the attitude I see more often in Christian circles is an odd mixture of guilt and anti-materialism that stifles ambition and the honest pursuit of good money. In many cases, I'm sure this stems from a sincere response to Jesus' warning: "For what does it profit a man to gain the whole world and forfeit his soul?"[48]

Let me be clear: I agree with Jesus. Do not pursue money in such a way or to the extent that you forget about the eternal implications of your present actions. We'll talk about this danger toward the end of the chapter. At the same time, do not use Bible verses about worldly gain to justify fear or laziness. Depending on your personal hang-ups, over the next few pages I want to give you permission—even challenge you—to make a decent living to the glory of God.

GOOD WORK, GOOD MONEY

I can tell you from personal experience, as I snapped photos of the Sweet and Sour Sisters at work, earning money is about so much more than money. Watching the girls put a plan together for something they wanted, and

---

48. Mark 8:36.

then following through with it, was very rewarding for me and valuable for them. Besides, they were incredibly cute, we got to meet some neighbors, and other parents and young entrepreneurs seemed to come out of the woodwork to cheer them on.

Money is a byproduct of work, not the goal of work. Human passion, drive, and ingenuity serve as an incredible testimony to the blessing and creativity of God, who gave us a mind we can use to accomplish amazing things. Though we can never out-build the God who fashioned the infinite expanse of the cosmos, the variety and scope of all that mankind has accomplished is nonetheless staggering, from art and athletic feats, to skyscrapers and space travel.

God made us to work, construct, and create, using money and the many other resources at our disposal. As tedious, soul-crushing, or meaningless as some jobs may seem, work is a gift from God, present in the garden of Eden even before sin entered into the world.[49] "The fact that God put work in paradise is startling to us because we so often think of work as a necessary evil or even punishment," Tim Keller writes. "Work is as much a basic human need as food, beauty, rest, friendship, prayer, and sexuality; it is not simply medicine but food for our soul. Without meaningful work we sense significant inner loss and emptiness."[50]

The characteristics that distinguish work as it was meant to be include:

49. Gen. 2:15.

50. Tim Keller, *Every Good Endeavor: Connecting Your Work to God's Work* (New York: Riverhead, 2012), 23.

- Honesty
- Diligent work ethic
- Competence gained from cultivating skills
- Maximizing (but not abusing) all available resources
- Fair, generous treatment of employees
- Making good use of your natural interests and abilities
- Loving consideration of other parties involved (co-workers, customers, suppliers, etc.)

Though we see these virtues celebrated throughout Scripture,[51] none of them are exclusive to Christians. Work is a gift from God that non-Christians can use and misuse, same as food, sex, nature, authority, and so on. As Professor Gene Edward Veith points out, however, Christians can enjoy the added bonus of knowing that "God himself works through human vocations in providential care as he governs the world. He provides daily bread through farmers and bakers. He protects us through lawful magistrates. He heals us by means of physicians, nurses, and pharmacists. He creates new life through mothers and fathers."[52]

In this way, all work is significant and filled with purpose. Veith continues:

51. Prov. 6:6–11, 10:2, 13:11, 20:21, 21:6, 28:20; Jer. 17:11; 1 Cor. 7:17; 1 Thess. 4:11; 2 Thess. 3:10.

52. Gene Edward Veith, "Which vocations should be off limits to Christians?," The Gospel Coalition, March 22, 2012, http://thegospelcoalition.org/article/which-vocations-should-be-off-limits-to-christians/.

Having been reconciled to God through Christ, we are then sent by God into the world to love and serve him by loving and serving our neighbors. This happens in vocation. So we can ask of every kind of work we are doing, "Am I loving and serving my neighbor, or am I exploiting and tempting him?"[53]

Another theologian, Anthony Bradley, provides a helpful summary of Veith's explanation of vocation:

This means that there are no little people in the Kingdom and no one has an insignificant career, job, or life. Being a bus driver is no less important than being a lawyer or a church planter in God's economy. What matters is that God's people are a love-driven people glorifying God wherever he places them.[54]

Since the primary purpose of work is not to make money, God dignifies non-paid jobs like homemakers and volunteers. "According to the Bible," Keller writes, "we don't merely need the money from work to survive; we need the work itself to survive and live fully human lives."[55]

For all Christians earning a paycheck, however, do not be afraid to try and make a lot of money. If you

53. Ibid.

54. Anthony Bradley, "Everyday Christianity: A Faith Free From The Accidental Pharisaism of Missional, Radical, Crazy and Other Superlatives," *Acton Institute Power Blog*, June 17, 2013, http://blog.acton.org/archives/56166-every-day-matters-liberation-from-the-shaming-accidental-pharisaism-of-missional-crazy-radical-and-superlative-christianities.html.

55. Keller, *Every Good Endeavor*, 25.

can generate significant income without making it your god, money in abundance can lead to great opportunities, freedom, and social good.

Money creates opportunities

It's sad when Christians err by not maximizing their opportunities. We see this mistake play out in the Parable of the Talents, where the "wicked and slothful"[56] servant is the one who buries his money instead of investing it because he's afraid to lose it.

Michael Hyatt, former CEO of publisher Thomas Nelson and blogger extraordinaire, goes so far as to say, "I believe I have a moral obligation to make as much money as I can. Why? Because there are people in need, and I have the opportunity to help them."[57]

Money opens doors, grabs attentions, and sparks change—all effective strategies whether in charity, business, community, or family life. As Hyatt says, "The more you make, the bigger impact you can have."[58]

Money provides freedom

Money can't buy happiness, salvation, love, or anything else that matters in life. Even pop music understands this (sort of). But there's no denying that a certain amount of money can provide greater flexibility and options in life.

Pat Flynn is one of the great success stories of the new Internet economy. After getting laid off in 2008, he

---

56. Matt. 25:26.

57. Michael Hyatt, "Why You Should Do It for the Money (and Stop Feeling Guilty About It)," *Michael Hyatt* (blog), October 11, 2013, http://michaelhyatt.com/do-it-for-the-money.html.

58. Ibid.

turned the roadblock into an opportunity and decided to create his own work by starting an online business. Fast forward a few years, and Pat is now the mogul of his own little media empire generating over $50,000 every month through ebooks, microsites, speaking gigs, blogs, and podcasts.

"It turns out that getting laid off was the best thing that ever happened to me," Pat writes on his website, SmartPassiveIncome.com. "Without my 9 to 5 job holding me back, I've since been able to earn more money and work less (and more flexible) hours—which in the end allows me to be home and spend time with my family."[59]

I've never met the guy, but Pat comes across as a humble, friendly guy who has discovered that money can be really great when it's not about the money. For anyone else willing to take a risk and work hard, the technology and trends emerging today offer more possibilities than ever. Failure comes with the territory, but when approached with humility and tenacity, roadblocks can become opportunities. Get to work, and hang in there.

Money accomplishes good

You don't need money to love your neighbor and do good in the world. Many people can and do accomplish far more with far less. But we would not have non-profit aid organizations, church buildings, disease research, and other humanitarian efforts unless somebody could pay the bills.

---

59. Pat Flynn, "About," *The Smart Passive Income Blog*, accessed October 1, 2014, http://www.smartpassiveincome.com/about/.

Bob Goff is a successful lawyer who refused to let the money get to his heart. In his best-selling, all-proceeds-donating book, *Love Does*, Bob calls his legal career "fund-raising."[60] As an attorney dealing with real estate and construction cases, Bob's day job is not explicitly "Christian," but his love for Jesus influences the way he goes about his work and what he does with the earnings. He made money and with it founded an organization called Restore International for "fighting injustices committed against children."[61] His paid work is "like a really successful bake sale to get rid of bad guys."[62]

In addition to generating funds for charitable efforts, building a successful business can bless the surrounding community simply through its existence. As entrepreneurs, investors, and leaders, "you see a human need not being met, you see a talent or resource that can meet that need, and you then invest your resources—at your risk and cost—so that the need is met and the result is new jobs, new products, and better quality of life."[63]

Mission doesn't happen without money, and money doesn't happen without a lot of planning, discipline, patience, reverse-engineering, study, and cooperation. Work hard, make money, and use it as an instrument to glorify God.

---

60. Bob Goff, *Love Does: Discover a Secretly Incredible Life in an Ordinary World* (Nashville, TN: Thomas Nelson, 2012), 204.

61. Ibid., 223.

62. Ibid., 204.

63. Keller, *Every Good Endeavor*, 50–51. Keller is recollecting a point from a lecture by Richard Mouw.

FINANCIAL SINS: COMMON MONEY MISTAKES

What's the downside? In his song, "Confessions," Lecrae recognizes the value of money, along with its accompanying dangers:

> *Ain't nothing wrong with havin' it, matter fact go and get it,*
> *But if you find identity in it then go 'n forget it.*
> *You gain the whole world but lost the only thing ya' own,*
> *'Cause everything else is just a temporary loan.*

For all its usefulness, money is still a trap. We may set out to make money with the best of intentions, and not even notice when we forget our role as stewards and become slaves instead, or worse. "How difficult it is for those who have wealth to enter the kingdom of God," Jesus said after an encounter with a man who chose riches over God. [64] Handle money with care, because "those who desire to be rich fall into temptation, into a snare, into many senseless and harmful desires that plunge people into ruin and destruction." [65]

Let's be honest. Mixed in with our practical, constructive, and benevolent motivations for making money, we desire something else in the process. We want to be rich because we want to control the future. We want to be rich because we want power over people. We want to be rich because we want comfort on earth now, not in heaven later. We want to be rich because we want to be like God.

---

64. Luke 18:24.

65. 1 Tim. 6:9.

Until we see Jesus face to face, money and our pursuit of it will lure us in this direction. You will be tempted to define yourself by what you build, or how much you make, or both. That's why guys like me can get caught up working to the neglect of my family at times. Beware of these other common financial sins in order to avoid "ruin and destruction":

- *Idolatry* –"You cannot serve God and money."[66]
- *Pride* –"When you give to the needy, sound no trumpet before you."[67]
- *Unnecessary debt* –"The borrower is the slave of the lender."[68]
- *Envy and covetousness* –"Envy makes the bones rot."[69]
- *No fear of the Lord* – "Better a little with the fear of the LORD than great treasure and trouble with it."[70]
- *Laziness* –"The sluggard craves and gets nothing."[71]
- *Lack of planning* –"Everyone who is hasty comes only to poverty."[72]
- *Greed* –"The love of money is a root of all kinds of evil."[73]

66. Matt. 6:24 cf. Luke 18:18–30.

67. Matt. 6:1–4.

68. Prov. 22:7.

69. Prov. 14:30 cf. Eccles. 4:4; Rom. 1:29.

70. Prov. 15:16.

71. Prov. 13:4 cf. 1 Tim. 5:8.

72. Prov. 21:5 cf. Prov. 15:21; 13:22; 19:14.

73. 1 Tim. 6:10 cf. 2 Kings 12:15–27; Acts 5:1–6.

- *False doctrine* – ". . . imagining that godliness is a means of gain."[74]
- *Not giving or tithing* – "Will man rob God? Yet you are robbing me. But you say, 'How have we robbed you?' In your tithes and contributions."[75]
- *Selfishness* – "You ask and do not receive, because you ask wrongly, to spend it on your passions."[76]
- *Hope in wealth* – "For you say, I am rich, I have prospered, and I need nothing."[77]
- *Seeking satisfaction in wealth* – "Whoever loves wealth is never satisfied with his income."[78]
- *Freeloading* – "If anyone is not willing to work, let him not eat."[79]
- *Worry* – "Do not be anxious about your life, what you will eat."[80]
- *Lack of vision* – "I was afraid, and I went and hid your talent in the ground."[81]
- *Entitlement* – "A person cannot receive even one thing unless it is given him from heaven."[82]

74. 1 Tim. 6:3–5.

75. Mal. 3:8.

76. James 4:3.

77. Rev. 3:17 cf. Luke 12:13–21; 1 Tim. 6:17–19; James 5:1–3.

78. Eccl. 5:10 (NIV) cf. 4:8.

79. 2 Thess. 3:6–15 cf. 1 John 3:17–18.

80. Luke 12:22–34.

81. Matt. 25:14–30.

82. John 3:27.

Make as much money as you need. Make more if you can. But do it for someone other than yourself, and always remember that true worth is found only in Jesus. [83] I need this reminder constantly. When I place work and money above family and faith, I'm thankful that Jesus is gracious to lead me back to a place of repentance and proper priorities. Whether you make a lot or a little, your work is valuable and meaningful as worship for him, not as validation for you.

83. Col. 3:3.

CHAPTER FIVE
SPEND IT

"Take care, and be on guard against all covetousness."
—Jesus [84]

I grew up in a family of big spenders. Credit cards were affectionately known as "free money cards" in our household, and as a rite of passage I got my own as soon as I turned 18. I took my freshly minted sheet of magical plastic straight to the electronics store and maxed out the $500 limit in less than an hour. I never felt so free!

One week later, however, my new stereo was stolen from my car, along with all of my CDs—at least $700 worth of the best butt-rock collection you've ever heard. I was so mad, but things got worse a few weeks later when my first statement showed up in the mail. I quickly learned that money isn't free after all. And neither was I. My stereo was gone, but I was still paying for it, plus interest, to fund some thief's road jams.

Like the Munson family once upon a time, debt is debilitating millions of Americans. The average credit card debt per household with a credit card is about $7,000. [85] In 2014, the average revolving debt for every man, woman,

---

84. Luke 12:15.

85. Fred O. Williams, "Average credit card debt statistics," CreditCards.com, July 8, 2013, http://www.creditcards.com/credit-card-news/average-credit_card_debt-1276.php.

and child in the country was about $2,700.[86] We spend on credit cards when we fail to plan, or when we covet things outside of our plan. These expenses usually seem harmless at the time, and we can easily rationalize spending beyond what we have:

- "It's a really good deal. I'm actually saving money."
- "I'll make sure to spend less next month to make up for this month's splurge."
- "Buying this thing will allow me to be more efficient and productive so I'll actually end up making more money."
- "It's been a tough day. I deserve to indulge."

Proverbs says, "The borrower is the slave of the lender."[87] Despite this warning, the temptation to spend, spend, spend is so strong that many of us close the shackles around our own wrists. Research findings published in 2013 "suggest that younger generations may continue to add credit card debt into their 70s, and die still owing money on their cards."[88]

Exorbitant consumer spending not only hampers our freedom, it also debilitates our ability to give, which in turn draws our hearts away from Jesus. Godly wisdom in spending is important not only because it honors the Lord,

---

86. "Consumer Credit – G.19, July 2014" FederalReserve.gov, September 8, 2014, http://www.federalreserve.gov/releases/g19/current/.

87. Prov. 22:7.

88. Jeff Grabmeier, "Credit card debt: Younger people borrow more heavily and repay more slowly, study finds," Phys.org, January 14, 2013, http://phys.org/news/2013-01-credit-card-debt-younger-people.html.

but also because it saves us from a life of slavery to the money god and his earthly treasures.

You will spend a lot of money over the course of your life. Rather than avoiding it or succumbing to it, we must learn how to spend wisely. This involves a paradigm shift, from wants and *needs* to wants and *priorities*.

YOU DON'T *NEED* MUCH OF ANYTHING

Air, food, and water. That's all I need.

Some may add clothing and shelter to the list, but I could run naked through the great outdoors and do just fine. I would probably need to re-locate to a milder climate and learn how to evade the authorities, but my life would not cease if I suddenly lost my house and then all my clothes disappeared.

We often separate desires into arbitrary categories of "wants" and "needs" to help us make decisions with our money. But this way of thinking can be problematic. In terms of purchases and possessions, almost nothing is technically a need. Therefore, honest attempts to manage your desires either lead to guilt (*My conscience won't let me eat anything besides tap water and vitamin paste*) or self-righteousness (*I do not indulge in luxuries such as lattes, Netflix, or anything fun*). You go see a movie and then feel bad about it because it's not vital for survival, or you avoid the cinema altogether and grow smug and judgmental against those who can't resist the latest comic book flick.

Also, avoiding wants leads to a negative focus—asceticism and self-denial—rather than a positive emphasis—on Jesus and his mission.[89] If you give up a latte per week in order to pay off debt or give more to your church, the focus is on you and what you should not do (buy a latte) rather than on God and what he's called you to do.

The other problem with wants and needs is that my list of wants is really, really, really long. I want a lot of things. For starters:

- I want to wear clothes.
- I want a roof over my head.
- I want to buy things for my family.
- I want to drive a car.
- I want to take my wife out on a date.
- I want a new phone.
- I want to take a vacation.
- I want to host our friends for dinner.

A straight-up comparison between my infinite wants list and my three-point needs list inevitably leads me to think in terms of guilt rather than grace. Rather than embracing the finished work of Jesus on my behalf, I begin to construct my own pathway to righteousness, wondering, "Which wants should I cut out in order to be a better Christian? How many can I keep and still be 'holy'?"

This mentality implicitly denies the gospel in favor of a list of rules that I must follow in order to alleviate guilt and condemnation. In the name of holiness we end up rejecting God's good gifts because anything remotely enjoyable or borderline indulgent stirs up remorse. Since we don't technically need a vacation, a deck, or a fancy dinner, some Christians suck it up and decline such gifts in blind devotion to austerity.

I'm not arguing against discernment, self-discipline, or moderation—a good steward must pursue all three—but if you're in the habit of always rejecting God's material blessings because they violate some arbitrary regulations, you're probably rejecting the fullness of his ultimate blessing as well: amazing grace. [90]

The truth is, I'm an imperfect sinner. I'm going to screw it up, which means that any guilt and condemnation I may feel aren't going anywhere—unless they're dealt with once and for all, which is exactly what Jesus did. "There is therefore now no condemnation for those who are in Christ Jesus." [91]

THE POWER OF PRIORITIZATION

Since the Bible does not draw any absolute distinctions between needs and wants. We're simply called to trust God for our needs [92] and be good stewards of everything else he provides. [93] Most wants are not inherently evil, but they are never-ending. Our resources, on the other hand, are finite, which means we must prioritize.

"The earth is the Lord's, and everything in it," [94] which means any want that doesn't involve breaking

---

90. Col. 2:20–3:4; Rom. 6:14.

91. Rom. 8:1.

92. Luke 12:24–25 cf. 11:13. We can trust him with our needs because God is a good and loving Father.

93. Matt. 25:21.

94. Psalm 24:1, NIV.

commandments can be justified. Therefore, our priorities actually determine how we spend our time, money, and energy on a daily basis. Jesus guides us through these decisions by the work of the Holy Spirit, the wisdom of Scripture, and the family of believers known as the church. Author and pastor Bill Clem explains how we follow Jesus "as redeemed image-bearers, worshipers, a community, and missionaries."[95] Each of these components of discipleship—identity, worship, community, and mission—carries with it God-given priorities that help us categorize our list of wants:

- *Prioritize Jesus.* Our identity is found in the person and work of Jesus, our Creator and Sustainer, Savior and King. Without him we are lost, so we must prioritize our relationship with him, and live our lives in worship of him.

- *Prioritize human relationships.* We were created to need one another, to love, serve, and help each other. Therefore, we must prioritize our relationships with people: our family, our church, our friends, and our neighbors.

- *Prioritize mission.* God has given us the mission to make disciples,[96] and he calls his disciples to participate in this work. We are entrusted with the message of Jesus[97]—we get to proclaim his work

95. Bill Clem, *Disciple: Getting Your Identity From Jesus* (Wheaton, IL: Crossway, 2011), 51.

96. Matt. 28:19; Acts 1:8.

97. 2 Cor. 5:20.

that saves people from death to life![98] Therefore, we must prioritize the gospel, using our resources to bless, care for, and share the gospel to those in our circles of influence.

Once we align our priorities according to life as a disciple, we can begin to evaluate our wants in light of this framework, and spend accordingly.

3 WAYS TO HONOR GOD IN SPENDING

Three additional considerations will inform the prioritization process and help us spend in a way that honors God.

1. Live within your means

Compulsive spenders commit themselves to more obligations than they have money to make good on, like me and my doomed car stereo. All of their money is gone before the paycheck even arrives. A 2013 survey of young renters found that 75 percent of these 18–24-year-olds outspend their income every month.[99] Spenders aren't always poor college students, however. Successful businessmen, pro athletes, and lottery winners often succumb to rash consumption.

Spenders wind up in trouble because they don't have the ability to maintain their chosen lifestyle. This

---

98. 2 Tim. 1:10.

99. Martha C. White, "Today's Young Adults Will Never Pay Off Their Credit Card Debts," *Business* (blog), *TIME*, January 17, 2013. http://business.time.com/2013/01/17/todays-young-adults-will-never-pay-off-their-credit-card-debts/.

leads to stress and fear, as their faith is "choked by the cares and riches and pleasures of life, and their fruit does not mature."[100] Over-spending and consumer debt are completely antithetical to the worship of a God who calls us to persevere, endure, and "bear fruit with patience."[101]

2. Don't be a hoarder

On the opposite end of the spectrum are the penny pinchers, the cheapskates, and the tightwads. Hoarders seek to maximize their savings. Like spenders, hoarders may have billions or nickels. In either case, hoarders are never satisfied with how much is in the bank. They tuck it away in fear or selfishness, building a financial stockpile for the rainiest of all rainy days.

I'm not opposed to savings, emergency funds, or investments, and we'll address these topics more in upcoming chapters. But hoarders place their faith in money as a lifeline, a security blanket, a mechanism of control, and a savior. They collect it, bury it, and obsess over it rather than putting it to use as a productive tool that can greatly benefit many others—never mind enjoying any of it as a gracious gift from God.

Jesus tells a story about three servants who each received a sum of money from their master before he left for some time. He returns to find that two of the servants put their gifts to use, doubling the value. The third servant, however, returns the original sum. "I was afraid," he confesses, "and I went and hid your [money] in the

100. Luke 8:14.

101. Luke 8:15.

ground."[102] The master is enraged and casts "the worthless servant into the outer darkness."[103]

God doesn't give us money so that it can replace him. He doesn't give us money so that we can admire the growing stash under the mattress. God gives us money in order to use it. The temptation to overspend is strong for many, but that doesn't mean we shouldn't spend at all. Like sex, food, drink, or any of God's gifts, it is possible to use money faithfully for great good and enjoyment.

3. Guard against covetousness

Like the instant gratification that fuels overspending, covetousness is widely accepted in our culture, and even seen as something of value. The late writer and prominent atheist Christopher Hitchens called *Thou shalt not covet* "the most questionable of the commandments." He supposed, "Is not envy a great spur to emulation and competition?"[104]

While there is a difference between healthy ambition[105] and covetousness, which is idolatry,[106] greed and envy are inevitable components of a consumer-driven economy, or any economy for that matter. The American Dream has devolved into one big covet-fest that empties

---

102. Matt. 25:25.

103. Matt. 25:30.

104. Christopher Hitchens, "The New Commandments," *Vanity Fair*, April 2010, http://www.vanityfair.com/culture/features/2010/04/hitchens-201004. Ecclesiastes 4:4 makes the same observation and calls such competition "vanity and a striving after wind."

105. See Dave Harvey, *Rescuing Ambition* (Wheaton, IL: Crossway, 2010).

106. Col. 3:5.

consumer wallets and then some. This is the water we swim in. We're already drenched and, unless we heed Jesus' words to "take care, and be on your guard against all covetousness,"[107] we'll drown and drag our families, our churches, and our communities to the bottom with us. The Great Recession that began in 2008 was in many ways a direct result of nationwide covetousness.

The temptation for more will never go away, but we indulge it at significant risk. For "it is through this craving that some have wandered away from the faith and pierced themselves with many pangs."[108] The alternative? "Now there is great gain in godliness with contentment, for we brought nothing into the world, and we cannot take anything out of the world."[109]

Such contentment requires the supernatural work of the Holy Spirit—especially for we the people of Western affluence. A good place to start is with the prayer found in Proverbs 30:

> Give me neither poverty nor riches;
> Feed me with the food that is needful for me,
> Lest I be full and deny you and say, "Who is the LORD?"
> Or lest I be poor and steal and profane the name
>   of my God.

You're going to spend. Remember contentment, moderation, and generosity, and then feel free to lighten

---

107. Luke 12:15.

108. 1 Tim. 6:10.

109. 1 Tim. 6:6–7.

up. Take your spouse out on a nice date. Plan a vacation for your family. Fix up your house. Throw a party. "There is room for the periodic celebration of God's good, material gifts, even at times to a lavish extent."[110] With guidance from the Holy Spirit and the Word, it is possible to spend money in a way that is neither selfish, nor frivolous, nor sinful—and even honors God.

IS GOD CALLING YOU TO GET A BIG SCREEN TV?

To illustrate some of the principles of godly spending, let's consider Doug. Doug is a disciple of Jesus with lots of non-Christian friends. Doug wants to buy a nice, big, new TV for many reasons, some righteous and some purely superficial. Yeah, he plans to invite his buddies over to watch sports, build relationships, offer hospitality, and point them to Jesus. But Doug also thinks it would be pretty relaxing and awesome to own a decent home entertainment system to enjoy on his own.

Is it wrong for Doug to drop a couple grand on home electronics?

It's easy for legalistic Christians to issue blanket condemnation of anything that costs a lot and therefore impedes "nobler" pursuits. Some even used this argument to criticize Jesus.[111] On the other hand, it's also easy for Christians to cite freedom in Christ to justify selfish, destructive behavior, making something a priority when it really should not be. If Doug can pay for a TV without going into debt, without compromising his ability to

110. Blomberg, *Neither Poverty nor Riches*, 145 cf. John 2:1–11, 15:23; Mark 14:3.
111. Matt. 26:8–9.

provide for his family, without turning it into trophy, and without ceasing to be a generous giver, then maybe Doug should buy a TV.

If Doug were thinking in terms of wants and needs, he would never buy the big screen. Or he would buy it and feel bad about spending money on something frivolous. In reality, some Dougs can buy their big screen, enjoy it for what it is, and even use it as a ministry tool, guilt-free. Amen. Other Dougs need to honor their higher priorities before reaching the big ticket items on their wants list.

Like all aspects of stewardship, spending is an act of worship that proceeds from a changed heart—not a rote list of dos and don'ts. The Bible gives us freedom, not a checklist, which compels us to rely on the Holy Spirit to provide discernment and wisdom, "For everything created by God is good, and nothing is to be rejected if it is received with thanksgiving, for it is made holy by the word of God and prayer."[112]

112. 1 Tim. 4:4–5.

CHAPTER SIX
SAVE IT

"The things you have prepared, whose will they be?"
—*God* [113]

Are you a rich fool?

Sounds harsh, I know. But consider Jesus' story about a wealthy man who did very well in his business, which happened to be farming. The man's crops went berserk and produced a bounty beyond what his existing infrastructure could contain. The guy literally had more currency than he knew what to do with. His solution sounds more than reasonable from our modern day perspective. "I will do this," he decides. "I will tear down my barns and build larger ones, and there I will store all my grain and my goods. And I will say to my soul, 'Soul, you have ample goods laid up for many years; relax, eat, drink, be merry.'" [114]

Unfortunately, the man failed to consider one important variable: God. The Lord hears the whole strategy and responds, "Fool! This night your soul is required of you, and the things you have prepared, whose will they be?" [115]

---

113. Luke 12:20.

114. Luke 12:18-19.

115. Luke 12:20.

After working hard to earn the good life, the rich man dies before he ever gets to enjoy the fruits of his labor. It's hard not to sympathize with the poor guy. Clearly he botched it, but his error raises a host of stewardship questions. Jesus graciously shares this example to teach us more about God's perspective on money, in particular when it comes to saving.

SAVING ISN'T SINFUL

We live in a world of unexpected car repairs, health insurance, and unprecedented longevity that generally concludes with steep end-of-life medical bills. To further complicate things, as a society we've compromised, undermined, and devalued the traditional safety nets of family and community. In this context, it would be foolish—and dangerous—to reject saving entirely. The lesson of the Rich Fool is not "don't save." In fact, the Bible offers numerous guidelines for how to save for the future in a way that honors God.

1. Save through hard work and preparation.

As we discussed in previous chapters, godly stewardship includes working to accumulate money and a plan for using it well. The parable of the Rich Fool is not a license to fly by the seat of our financial pants or let cash stream through our fingers the minute it reaches our hands. On the contrary, the Bible celebrates the value of long-term planning, especially in the book of Proverbs:

- "Go to the ant, O sluggard; consider her ways, and be wise . . . she prepares her bread in summer and gathers her food in harvest."[116]
- "Wealth gained hastily will dwindle, but whoever gathers little by little will increase it."[117]
- "The plans of the diligent lead surely to abundance, but everyone who is hasty comes only to poverty."[118]
- "Prepare your work outside; get everything ready for yourself in the field, and after that build your house."[119]

2. Trust in God, not your savings.

The error of the Rich Fool is not his attempt to plan for the future, but his presumptuous, self-absorbed perspective on the future. He operates as an owner instead of a steward, believing as so many of us do that he can actually control the events and outcomes of his life. In other words, his sin is pride. The book of James makes this diagnosis plain:

> Come now, you who say, "Today or tomorrow we will go into such and such a town and spend a year there and trade and make a profit"—You do not know what tomorrow will bring. What is your life? For you are a mist that appears for a little time and then vanishes . . .

---

116. Prov. 6:6, 8.

117. Prov. 13:11.

118. Prov. 21:5.

119. Prov. 24:27.

As it is, you boast in your arrogance. All such boasting is evil. [120]

In contrast, the Bible includes other examples of wealthy yet humble men who face unexpected calamities that disrupt best-laid plans. Job had it made before God allowed Satan to take everything, including Job's ten children and all of his wealth. Job spends 40 chapters grieving over his tragic life, but ultimately he accepts his position as a mere man, not a god who can exercise sovereign will despite great earthly power and status. "The LORD gave, and the LORD has taken away," Job says. "Blessed be the name of the LORD." [121] Job certainly would have preferred a life of prosperity over a life of ruin, but prosperity was not his god or savior.

Another example shows up in parable form when Jesus tells the story of two men who build houses. One builds on rock and the other builds on sand. Both experience severe storms, and only the house on the rock survives. The difference? Jesus says, "Everyone who hears these words of mine and does not do them will be like a foolish man who built his house on the sand." [122] All of our saving, preparation, and plans amount to nothing if these contingencies replace God as the bedrock of our life and hope.

120. James 4:13–14, 16.

121. Job 1:21.

122. Matt. 7:26.

3. Save without anxiety.

Save as an act of prudence and stewardship, not as an act of anxiety and fear of what the future may hold.[123] God does not require us to save, but he does require us to trust him because only he can truly provide what we need both now and through eternity.

4. Save for a godly purpose.

The Rich Fool saved up to indulge himself. Once again, James has strong words for this kind of strategy. "You have laid up treasure in the last days," James rebukes the unrighteous rich. "You have lived on the earth in luxury and in self-indulgence. You have fattened your hearts in a day of slaughter."[124]

God has no tolerance for our efforts to create our own personal heaven on earth in the form of physical comfort, financial security, and luxurious pleasures. Not only does this selfish approach numb us to the cares and concerns of the world we're called to love and serve—a "fattened heart" is insulated from empathy—we're on unstable sand when our hope resides in created things instead of the Creator God.[125] There is a dangerous difference between enjoying God's gifts in worship to him, and worshiping God's gifts to enjoy ourselves.

If your objective in saving is solely to accrue wealth, you may "fall into temptation, into a snare, into many senseless and harmful desires that plunge people

123. Luke 12:22–34.

124. James 5:3, 5-6.

125. Rom. 1:25.

into ruin and destruction."[126] The apostle Paul offers an alternative to compound luxury. He challenges the rich to use their resources "to do good, to be rich in good works, to be generous and ready to share."[127]

"God's people may at times be enormously wealthy," writes Craig Blomberg, "but a major purpose of God granting them wealth is that they may share it with those in need."[128] The Rich Fool took his wealth to be his own, not a gift from God. When he died, he lost everything. Those who focus on others, however, giving, saving, and spending to honor God, grow rich toward him. When they die, they will gain everything.[129] Generosity is the ultimate investment, as we will learn in the coming chapters.

PEOPLE AREN'T MADE TO RETIRE

The Rich Fool's scenario painfully resembles our contemporary notion of retirement. What's a godly, aging steward to do with this predicament?

The word "retirement" is not in the Bible, but faithfully saving money over the course of a lifetime and reaching a point where you can quit your day job is not a bad thing, provided your post-career years are spent living for Jesus, not just comfort and ease. Such a transition could in fact be a great gift if the extra time is used to

---

126. 1 Tim. 6:9.

127. 1 Tim. 6:18 cf. 5:8.

128. Blomberg, *Neither Poverty nor Riches*, 59.

129. Col. 3:1–4.

invest in family, serve others with your gifts, and help those God brings into your life.

It's not a sin to enjoy golf, naps, and other good things God has given at any particular point in life, but he didn't create us to hit cruise control at age sixty-five. As we discussed in chapter four, work is a gift from God, and even Adam had a job, to work and keep the Garden of Eden.[130] Though work became laborious toil after the Fall,[131] that doesn't change the fact that we were built to work, finish the race,[132] and bring glory to God in doing so.[133] Exactly what work looks like, however, will change with age, energy, and financial needs.

Take Rick Warren, for example. After writing one of the best-selling books in the history of the world,[134] he decided to retire from staff at the church he founded: Saddleback, congregation 20,000-plus. "I could have bought an island," he says, "and had people serve me little drinks of iced tea with umbrellas in them the rest of my life." Instead, Pastor Rick paid back his salary from twenty-five years of ministry and continues his work at Saddleback as a volunteer. He now gives away over 90 percent of his income.[135]

---

130. Gen. 2:15.

131. Gen. 3:17–19.

132. 1 Cor. 9:24–27.

133. 1 Cor. 10:31.

134. PurposeDrivenLife.com, "About The Author," accessed October 10, 2010, http://www.purposedrivenlife.com/en-US/AboutUs/AboutTheAuthor/About-TheAuthor.htm.

135. Rick Warren, "Radical Generosity," (lecture, Saddleback Church, Lake Forest, CA, February 12, 2010).

Few of us will need to worry about what to do with extraordinary wealth, but of course stewardship has little to do with the totals and everything to do with the heart. You don't need a lot of money to be as generous as Rick Warren or as shortsighted as the Rich Fool. How much we can give, save, and spend will vary from season to season. We may not always be able to do as much as we'd like, but don't make that an excuse to give up on diligence. Pray and plan in order to make sustained improvement and progress over a long period of time.

To paraphrase author and pastor Randy Alcorn, God grants retirement not to raise your standard of living, but to raise your standard of giving.[136] Whatever you're saving for, remember to be "rich toward God" and store up treasure for heaven, not treasure for yourself.[137]

---

136. Alcorn, *The Treasure Principle*, 75.

137. Luke 12:21.

CHAPTER SEVEN

INVEST IT

*"Provide yourselves with moneybags that do not grow old,
with a treasure in the heavens that does not fail."*
—Jesus [138]

What if I told you about an investment deal that could
provide a return so enormous, you'd never have to worry
about money again? In fact, the return on this investment
would be significant enough to fulfill all of your deepest
longings and desires. And what if I told you that I got this
hot tip from a guy who has never been wrong?

What's the catch? As with any investment, this one
comes with a risk commensurate to the reward: you invest
by giving away your money, and the full payoff won't
happen until after you die.

THE ETERNAL PROSPECTUS

Jesus says we can gain treasure in heaven by giving our
time, energy, money, and skills to seek the kingdom of
God. This is the opposite of how the world operates. "For
all the nations of the world seek after these things," Jesus
says, referring to material possessions, "and your Father

138. Luke 12:33.

knows that you need them. Instead, seek his kingdom, and these things will be added to you."[139]

God is good and he makes good things, in heaven and on earth. When Jesus discourages us from storing up earthly treasures, he's not saying that money and possessions are bad. They simply won't last.

Keep your treasure on earth and you'll lose it in the end, because here "moth and rust destroy and . . . thieves break in and steal."[140] Give your treasure away, however, and you'll never lose it. Like salvation for those who love Jesus, your treasure will be kept "where no thief approaches and no moth destroys."[141] Randy Alcorn calls it the Treasure Principle: You can't take it with you—but you can send it on ahead.[142]

"It's not an emotional appeal," explains Alcorn, "it's a logical one: Invest in what has lasting value. . . . Whatever treasure we store up on earth will be left behind when we leave. Whatever treasures we store up in heaven will be waiting for us when we arrive."[143]

WHAT IS "TREASURE IN HEAVEN"?

The Bible does not downplay the fact that heaven includes great rewards, and that eternity will ultimately be a physical existence complete with the best of the best. After

---

139. Luke 12:30–31.

140. Matt. 6:19.

141. Luke 12:33.

142. Alcorn, *The Treasure Principle*, 18.

143. Alcorn, *The Treasure Principle*, 19.

a life-changing encounter with Jesus, the Apostle Paul invested his entire life in eternity. "For I am already being poured out as a drink offering, and the time of my departure has come," he writes toward the end:

> I have fought the good fight, I have finished the race, I have kept the faith. Henceforth there is laid up for me the crown of righteousness, which the Lord, the righteous judge, will award to me on that Day, and not only to me but also to all who have loved his appearing.[144]

Peter also looked forward to "an inheritance that is imperishable, undefiled, and unfading, kept in heaven."[145] This inheritance awaits all who have been "born again to a living hope through the resurrection of Jesus Christ from the dead."[146]

In addition to the treasures of salvation and eternal life enjoyed by all believers, the Bible promises additional heavenly rewards, distributed according to how we conduct ourselves on earth.[147] The promise of treasure should serve as some encouragement—incentive even— for Christians to persevere. "I beat my body and make it my slave," Paul explains, "so that after I have preached to others, I myself will not be disqualified for the prize."[148]

144. 2 Tim. 4:6–8.

145. 1 Peter 1:4.

146. 1 Peter 1:3.

147. Matt. 6:6, 18; Luke 6:23, 35; 1 Cor. 3:14.

148. 1 Cor. 9:27.

Since none of us have ever been to heaven, banking on this investment takes supernatural faith that only the Holy Spirit can provide. None of us can say how the whole treasure distribution system will actually take place, let alone the precise nature of these mysterious rewards. The fact that God will be there provides some clue, however. "In view of God's infinite power and wisdom and beauty," Pastor John Piper says, "What could God give us to enjoy that would prove him most loving? There is only one possible answer: Himself! . . . He alone can satisfy the heart's longing to be happy."[149]

But if we're motivated to give by what we'll receive in return, isn't that selfish? What difference does it make if the payoff is delayed until the next life? Piper has some helpful thoughts on this as well:

> The reason our generosity toward others is not a sham love when we are motivated by the longing for God's promise is that we are aiming to take those others with us into that reward. We know our joy in heaven will be far greater if the people we treat with mercy are won over to the surpassing worth of Christ and join us in praising Him. . . .
>
> It would only be unloving if we pursued our joy at the expense of others. But if our very pursuit includes the pursuit of their joy, how is that selfish? How am I the less loving to you if my longing for God moves

149. John Piper, *Desiring God: Meditations of a Christian Hedonist* (Colorado Springs: Multnomah, 2003), 47–48, 96.

me to give away my earthly possessions so that my joy in Him can be forever doubled in your partnership of praise?[150]

When the Christian gives to gain more of God, everybody wins. In our sinful state, it is difficult to comprehend a scenario where it's healthy to desire something in return for our giving. Consider the alternative, however, and it all begins to make a bit more sense. John Piper, one more time:

> The one who actually sets himself above God is the person who presumes to come to God to give rather than get. With a pretense of self-denial, he positions himself as God's benefactor—as if the world and all it contains were not already God's (Psalm 50:12)! . . . You cannot please God if you do not come to him for reward! [Heb. 11:6] . . . He is our exceeding great reward! In his presence is fullness of joy, and at his right hand are pleasures forevermore. [Ps. 16:11][151]

It's also encouraging to remember that this "exceeding great reward" and all of the treasures in heaven are equally accessible to everyone. How much you give counts for nothing. What matters is generosity "according to what a person has, not according to what he does not

---

150. Piper, *Desiring God*, 195–196.

151. Ibid., 95, 102.

have."[152] That's how an old woman with two pennies can give more than any rich man. [153]

God asks us to live generously with what we have. Not with what we don't have, and not with what our neighbors have. The scope is intensely personal, aimed right at the heart.

HEAVEN PRACTICE STARTS NOW

Money follows heart. Heart follows money. The more you invest—money, time, energy—in Jesus' mission on earth, the more you'll look forward to seeing everything come to fruition when Jesus returns. In the process, giving generously will compel you to part with stuff that you might otherwise be tempted to worship, trust, and cling to—stuff that could choke out[154] the hope of Jesus' great promise: "It is your Father's good pleasure to give you the kingdom."[155]

In the book of Revelation, John describes the scene in heaven when the kingdom of God is complete. The people of God, forgiven, redeemed, and made righteous by Jesus, celebrate in his presence together:

> Then I heard what seemed to be the voice of a great multitude, like the roar of many waters and like the sound of mighty peals of thunder, crying out,

---

152. 2 Cor. 8:12.

153. Luke 21:3–4.

154. Luke 8:14.

155. Luke 12:32.

"Hallelujah! For the Lord our God the Almighty
reigns. Let us rejoice and exult and give him the glory,
For the marriage of the Lamb has come, and his Bride has
made herself ready; it was granted her to clothe herself
with fine linen, bright and pure" . . .

Blessed are those who are invited to the
marriage supper of the Lamb.[156]

Here is the ultimate fulfillment of the provision
Jesus promises when he says, "Do not be anxious about your
life, what you will eat, nor about your body, what you will
put on."[157] In the end, we will have plenty of clothes—fine
linen, bright and pure. In the end, we will have plenty of
food at the marriage supper of Jesus. Though "in this world
you will have trouble,"[158] God will ultimately make good on
his word to provide everything we need and more, tangibly
and for all time.

This heavenly treasure may still seem far off in the
distant future, but we have forgiveness of sins today. We
have the free gift of grace today. We have the Holy Spirit
today. Already "the kingdom of God has come upon you,"[159]
and though it's not yet time for the marriage feast of the
Lamb, the countdown has begun, and our invitation could
arrive at any moment. In the meantime, it's our great privilege, mission, joy, and treasure to invite others to the party,
and buy into this investment opportunity to end all others.

---

156. Rev. 19:6–9.

157. Luke 12:22.

158. John 16:33 (NIV).

159. Luke 11:20.

TOO GOOD TO BE TRUE?

Storing up treasure in heaven and growing rich toward God requires patience and delayed gratification—laughable concepts in the Google Age, yet sound practice for any investment. Is it worth it? Can it be true?

By faith, the best I can say is . . . I think so. But I will tell you with absolute certainty that life as we know it will someday end in death, and we'll leave behind anything we've invested in this world. Heaven sounds like a much safer, better place to put my money, but you don't have to take my word for it. Listen to Jesus: "The kingdom of heaven is like treasure hidden in a field, which a man found and covered up. Then in his joy he goes and sells all that he has and buys that field."[160]

The potential is both exciting and daunting, and don't expect to play it safe somewhere in between. "The rule of kingdom investment, however, is all or nothing," writes Ed Welch. "All hedged bets are deposited in the earthly kingdom—the one with 'mine' written all over it. Everything must go into one account or the other."[161] As Jesus said, "Whoever seeks to preserve his life will lose it, but whoever loses his life will keep it."[162]

Inevitably, we'll get cold feet and make mistakes along the way. We'll "buy high and sell low," whatever the spiritual equivalent of that blunder may be. "Confession

---

160. Matt. 13:44.

161. Welch, *Running Scared*, 163.

162. Luke 17:33.

acknowledges that we still invest in both kingdoms, hoping to minimize our risk," as Welch puts it. [163]

Thankfully, our God is more gracious and forgiving than any trustee or CEO. And generosity is the means to treasure in heaven, not a means to get into heaven. Jesus is the only way we can buy into this whole opportunity. We must receive his generous gift of grace and forgiveness before our investment gift counts for anything.

GIVE WHAT YOU CANNOT KEEP

In 1956, a Christian missionary named Jim Elliot was speared to death in the jungles of South America while ministering to a violent indigenous tribe. Four of his colleagues died in the same attack. The men were armed with guns, but chose to die rather than fire on the people God had called them to serve.

Jim was 28 at the time, and left behind a wife and a baby girl. His death was tragic by any measure. From a conventional perspective, it was also foolish. After all, he deliberately put himself in a very dangerous situation and experienced the natural consequence. But Jim was well aware of this potential, and chose to sacrifice anyway. An entry from his journal on October 28, 1949, suggests why. Jim wrote, "He is no fool who gives what he cannot keep to gain that which he cannot lose." [164]

163. Welch, *Running Scared*, 163.

164. Billy Graham Center Archives, "Jim Elliot Quote," October 10, 2010, http://www.wheaton.edu/bgc/archives/faq/20.htm.

Jim Elliot made an investment in the kingdom larger than most of us will ever make. Everyday investors can still learn from his example, however. Keep what you have and lose it in the end. Give what you have and enjoy much more in return.

CHAPTER EIGHT
GIVE IT

"Sell your possessions, and give to the needy."
—Jesus [165]

This chapter may very well be the most important section of this entire book. In *Contagious Generosity*, Chris Willard and Jim Sheppard describe the tremendous implications of what it means to give our money:

> Generosity is the fullest expression of the life of a steward, one who has been given a gift that must be used wisely and for a purpose, bringing glory to God. . . . It expresses in practical and powerful ways the message at the core of our faith: God gave his only Son to us that we might have life. [166]

Because most of the world holds money so dear, people often take notice and even get confused when we give it away. Try it some time (see page 89 for spontaneous generosity ideas). You'll be amazed, and possibly entertained, by the reactions you see.

---

165. Luke 12:33.

166. Chris Willard and Jim Sheppard, *Contagious Generosity: Creating a Culture of Giving in Your Church* (Grand Rapids, MI: Zondervan, 2012), 19–20.

GOOD REASONS TO GIVE

As we learned from the poor widow and her two coins, *why* you give matters more than *how much* you give.[167] The Bible provides a number of reasons to be generous. Here are a few, in no particular order:

Give because you are made in the image of God.
Author Gordon MacDonald describes how each member of the Trinity demonstrates generosity, "God the Father is the first generous giver, God the Son is the chief of generous givers, and God the Holy Spirit is the ongoing expression of God's generosity in us."[168] As God's image-bearers[169] we bear his imprint, which includes an inherent sense that generosity is good.

John 3:16 says, "For God so loved the world, that he *gave* his only Son, that whoever believes in him should not perish but have eternal life" (emphasis added). Pastor and author Judah Smith points out that God did not reference his heavenly spreadsheet and create a plan of salvation based on economic efficiency. The Bible does not say, "For God thought it was best and most reasonable, that he gave." No, it was because God so *loved* the world, that he gave. He is the original cheerful giver. When we give, we reflect that joy.[170]

---

167. Luke 21:1–4. See chapter 2.

168. Gordon MacDonald, *Generosity* (Alpharetta, GA: The National Christian Foundation, 2009), 6.

169. Gen. 1:27.

170. Judah Smith, "Swallow Your Saliva" (sermon), June 8, 2014, http://thecity.org/message/swallow_your_saliva.

Give as an act of praise to God.

The most appropriate response to this exorbitant generosity is generosity. We say "thank you" to God in part by giving to others. God gives life, provision, grace, and salvation. He gives children to parents, husbands to wives, and wives to husbands. He gives Christians the Holy Spirit. He gives comfort and prayer, faith and hope, wisdom and love. He gives us everything we have here on earth, and he adopts us into his family to give us everything he has in eternity.

Give to demonstrate the value of Jesus.

Those who love Jesus have even more reason to emulate his example of generosity.[171] Every opportunity to give becomes an opportunity to demonstrate that our truest, most valuable possession is Jesus and the hope we have in him. "If stewardship is a sign of a redeemed life, then Christians will, by their new natures, want to give."[172]

Give to be blessed.

If all of this weren't reason enough to be generous, Jesus said, "It is more blessed to give than to receive."[173] Not that it always feels that way. "The grace of God makes Christ precious to us, so that our possessions, our money, our time have all become eternally and utterly expendable,"

---

171. 2 Cor. 8:9.

172. Craig L. Blomberg, *Neither Poverty nor Riches*, 247.

173. Acts 20:35.

writes Tim Keller. "They used to be crucial to our happiness. They are not so now."[174]

As Keller observes, possessions, money, and time often do seem crucial to our happiness. We are not blessed because of the warm, fuzzy feeling that comes from doing something nice for somebody. We are not blessed because we will receive $1,000 for every $100 we give (reread chapter 2 on prosperity theology if you approach giving like a pyramid scheme). We are more blessed because giving "breaks us out of orbit around our possessions," explains Randy Alcorn. "We escape their gravity, entering a new orbit around our treasures in heaven."[175]

Give to care for others.

Jesus tells us to "seek first the kingdom of God and his righteousness, and all these things will be added to you."[176] By "these things," he's referring to essentials like food, water, and clothes. This supernatural provision often takes place as God works through his people. "As the community of the redeemed seeks first God's righteous standards, by definition they will help the needy in their midst," Craig Blomberg observes.[177] And "when believers realize that others will care for them if they unexpectedly find themselves impoverished, they can then be freed to give more generously in times of plenty."[178]

174. Timothy J. Keller, *Ministries of Mercy* (Phillipsburg, NJ: P&R Publishing, 1997), 63.

175. Randy Alcorn, *The Treasure Principle*, 34.

176. Matt. 6:33.

177. Blomberg, *Neither Poverty nor Riches*, 132.

178. Ibid., 145.

The book of Acts provides an example of what this looks like. "There was not a needy person among" the early Christians. [179] This pattern continued, and extended beyond the family of believers. In A.D. 361, Roman emperor Julian complained that "the impious Galileans [Christians, 'impious' because they did not conform to the pagan practices of the day] support both their own poor and ours as well; all men see that our people lack aid from us!" [180]

Give to serve Jesus.

According to Jesus himself, at the end of time he will ascend his throne and separate people into two groups: the sheep and the goats. The sheep will be invited to "inherit the kingdom." To the goats, however, he says, "Depart from me." [181] He explains to the sheep, "I was hungry and you gave me food, I was thirsty and you gave me drink, I was a stranger and you welcomed me, I was naked and you clothed me, I was sick and you visited me, I was in prison and you came to me." [182] The goats did none of these things.

Both groups are confused by Jesus' recollection. They ask, "Lord, when did we see you hungry and feed you, or thirsty and give you drink?" [183] When we ask the

179. Acts 4:34.

180. Quoted in Keller, *Ministries of Mercy*, 87.

181. Matt. 25:34, 41.

182. Matt. 25:35–36.

183. Matt. 25:37.

same question someday, Jesus will answer, "Truly, I say to you, as you did it to one of the least of these my brothers, you did it to me."[184] God does not need our giving.[185] Our giving serves as a test of whether we need him.

Giving to the glory of God reveals our true allegiance, along with his lavish love, generous grace, humble power, and faithful promises for the world.

BAD REASONS TO GIVE

Any act of generosity expresses shades of truth. A desire to do good, show mercy, and work for justice[186] reveals God's imprint on our hearts. God created us for good works.[187] Giving that serves to heal the sick, feed the hungry, and promote justice provides a picture of the kingdom of God.[188]

But God is not pleased by any gift for any reason. On a number of occasions in both the Old and New Testaments, God rejects the sacrifice of his people, due to their hypocrisy, half-heartedness, and pretentious motives.[189] Our natural desire to give is affected by sin, and any act of benevolence we attempt is compromised by pride. We cannot please God in and of ourselves.[190] Only through

---

184. Matt. 25:40.

185. Ps. 50:9–11.

186. Micah 6:8.

187. Eph. 2:10.

188. Luke 7:5.

189. For examples, see Gen. 4:5; Ps. 51:16–17; Is. 1:13; Amos 5:21–22; Mal. 1:6–14; Matt. 6:2; Acts 5:1–11.

190. Rom. 8:8.

Jesus can our gifts be made acceptable to God, allowing us to avoid the following common pitfalls.

Don't give to buy God's favor.

When giving proceeds from an unredeemed heart, it serves to nurture human pride, self-sufficiency, and morality, drawing us away from God rather than toward him. Generosity is meant to spill out of our worship and love for him, not complete a karmic transaction that moves us one notch closer to holiness.

Warren Buffett summarized the common, if often unspoken, belief that we can buy God's love. After donating $30 billion to the Gates Foundation he said, "There is more than one way to get to heaven, but this is a great way."[191] On the contrary, the Bible teaches, "For by grace you have been saved through faith. And this is not your own doing; it is the gift of God, not a result of works, so that no one may boast."[192]

Don't give to win glory.

Scroll through the list of billionaire philanthropists on The Giving Pledge website (givingpledge.org) and see how many are vested in foundations and programs named after

---

191. "Warren Buffett signs over $30.7B to Bill and Melinda Gates Foundation," *USA Today*, June 26, 2006, http://www.usatoday.com/money/2006-06-25-buffett-charity_x.htm. He later tried to clarify his statement, but the underlying sentiment remains evident throughout American culture and religion: the way to get to heaven is by being a good person (Bob Gary, Jr., "Billionaire clarifies 'get to heaven' remarks," Chattanooga Times and Free Press, July 12, 2006, http://www.allbusiness.com/society-social-assistance-lifestyle/philanthropy-charities/14639689-1.html).

192. Eph. 2:8–9.

themselves. The über wealthy aren't the only ones liable to twist generosity for some personal boost, however.

C. S. Lewis observes, "Sometimes our pride also hinders our charity; we are tempted to spend more than we ought on the showy forms of generosity (tipping, hospitality) and less than we ought on those who really need our help."[193]

Conspicuous benevolence is also common on social media, where your $10 contribution to a particular organization allows the world to see how much you care. Whether it's a grateful smile from the barista, a dozen Likes on our Facebook page, or our name in the charity's title, we give to get accolades, gratitude, applause, and recognition.

To put it plainly, we want the worship only God deserves. We are glory thieves. None of it belongs to us, however, "for when [a man] dies he will carry nothing away; his glory will not go down after him."[194] If you give for a pat on the back, that's all the glory you can expect to get. As Jesus says, "Thus, when you give to the needy, sound no trumpet before you, as the hypocrites do in the synagogues and in the streets, that they may be praised by others. Truly, I say to you, they have received their reward."[195]

Rather, if you want to glorify God with your giving, "do not let your left hand know what your right

---

193. C.S. Lewis, *Mere Christianity* (New York: HarperCollins, 2001), 86–87.

194. Ps. 49:17.

195. Matt. 6:2.

hand is doing, so that your giving may be in secret. And your Father who sees in secret will reward you." [196]

Don't give as an afterthought.

Lots of people are generous—when it's convenient. According to the leading research on Christian giving, 20 percent of all U.S. Christians give nothing to church, parachurch, or nonreligious charities, [197] and the vast majority give "very little." [198] But God requires the "first-fruits" of our labor, [199] without qualification. He loves us and wants us to trust in him and not our money.

A couple in our church was facing steep medical bills after a serious car wreck. They met with a non-Christian legal counselor whose first piece of advice was to stop giving to the church. They opted not to take his advice. A few months after the accident, the couple's Bible study group organized a fundraiser that provided an extra $4,000 toward medical expenses. Many people were blessed by this tangible demonstration of Jesus' love among his people, and at least one man became a Christian in response! The Father proved faithful, and the couple was able to receive God's gift without guilt or shame.

Don't give out of guilt.

In his book *Ministries of Mercy*, Tim Keller writes this insightful passage explaining the motivation for Christian

196. Matt. 6:3–4.

197. Christian Smith, Michael O. Emerson, and Patricia Snell, *Passing the Plate* (New York: Oxford University Press, 2008), 29.

198. Ibid., 34.

199. Prov. 3:9.

generosity by contrasting it with another very common yet fundamentally flawed tactic:

> Often books and speakers tell Christians that they should help the needy because they have so much . . . Ultimately it produces guilt. It says, "How selfish you are to eat steak and drive two cars when the rest of the world is starving!" This creates great emotional conflicts in the hearts of Christians who hear such arguing. We feel guilty, but all sorts of defense mechanisms are engaged. "Can I help it I was born in this country? How will it really help anyone if I stop driving two cars? Don't I have the right to enjoy the fruits of my labor?" Soon, with an anxious weariness, we turn away from books or speakers who simply make us feel guilty about the needy.
>
> The Bible does not use guilt-producing motivation. . . . The deeper the experience of the free grace of God, the more generous we must become. This is why Robert Murray M'Cheyne could say: "There are many hearing me who now know well that they are not Christians because they do not love to give. To give largely and liberally, not grudging at all, requires a new heart."[200]

Godly generosity is an outward sign of inward transformation: rebirth by the power of the Holy Spirit. It is quite possible to give tremendous sums to worthy causes and offend God in the process, if we operate out of

200. Keller, *Ministries of Mercy*, 62–63.

self-righteousness ("according to the flesh," as Romans 8:4 says) rather than the righteousness God gives us through Jesus. "Those who are in the flesh cannot please God."[201] If we live "according to the Spirit," however, we can live generous lives that please God.[202]

3 CHARACTERISTICS OF A GENEROUS ATTITUDE

God wants our hearts more than our money, which means our attitude matters in addition to our motives.

In 2 Corinthians, Paul writes about a church in Macedonia that loves to give. When a need in Jerusalem arose, the Macedonians began "begging us earnestly for the favor of taking part in the relief of the saints."[203] In commenting on this passage, Ralph Martin says, "Normally we think of the fundraiser as 'begging' the would-be donors. Here it is the donors, who could least afford it, who entreated Paul for the favor of having a part in this enterprise."[204]

Paul draws many helpful principles from the Macedonians' example. In short, an attitude of godly generosity is demonstrated by giving that is cheerful, sacrificial, and regular.

Cheerful giving

"Each one must give as he has decided in his heart, not reluctantly or under compulsion, for God loves a cheerful

201. Rom. 8:8.

202. Rom. 8:4.

203. 2 Cor. 8:4.

204. Quoted in Blomberg, *Neither Poverty nor Riches*, 192.

giver."[205] Money is a useful tool that God gives us to help others and spread the gospel. When we use it in this way, more people are served, more people meet Jesus, more people move from death to life, and more people enjoy the same grace that has been given to us.

When our church opened a new location in 2010, it was a huge party and dozens got baptized on the spot. It was an incredibly joyful celebration made possible by the many people who gave the resources that allowed us to buy the building, support the pastor, and pay the bills. When you're excited to see Jesus change lives, you get excited to play a part by giving. It's not a chore; it's an honor.

If God loves a cheerful giver, does that mean he doesn't love a grumpy giver? "No," says Judah Smith. "He loves the grouch that gives. But what this does mean is God gets a kick out of people who really like giving [. . .] because he is a cheerful giver. This is who he is."[206] Compulsion plays no part in the kingdom of God. Rather, "when he touches your heart, your hand just opens."[207]

Sacrificial giving

Paul also applauds the Macedonian congregation for giving to a church in need, despite the fact that the Macedonians themselves were in the middle of hard times. Despite hardship, "their abundance of joy and their extreme poverty have overflowed in a wealth of

---

205. 2 Cor. 9:7.

206. Smith, "Swallow Your Saliva." See John 3:16, also referenced above.

207. Ibid.

generosity."[208] Paul draws a connection between this sacrifice and the ultimate sacrifice of Jesus, who willingly sacrificed his life in order to serve and save sinners.

Our giving cannot equal Jesus' giving, but it's clear that, as his disciples, we are to contribute in similar sacrificial fashion. As opposed to giving out of excess, we willingly give up something we could have had in order to take part in giving to support God's work and mission.

Regular giving

The Bible does not mandate a specific frequency, day, or time for giving. We have freedom to establish a consistent plan that matches the rhythm of our lives. Regular giving requires us to live a disciplined life and also serves as a constant reminder that what we have does not actually belong to us. Irregular giving indicates poor stewardship: a reluctance to give, lack of planning, or laziness. Of course, regular giving does not rule out spontaneous giving, as we'll discuss later on.

To summarize the principles of generous, godly giving:

Giving Principle	If present ...	If absent ...
Cheerful	Excitement and joy to participate in the work of Jesus.	Giving feels like a loss and not a privileged gain.

208. 2 Cor. 8:2.

83

Giving Principle	If present . . .	If absent . . .
Sacrificial	Giving hurts a bit. It requires going without something.	Lack of faith and trust in God's provision. Other priorities take precedent over God.
Regular	Giving occurs on a consistent basis.	Laziness, poor planning, and indifference lead to sporadic giving (usually guilt-based).

THE BOTTOM LINE: HOW MUCH?

Regardless of what the Bible says about cheerfulness and sacrifice, the little legalist inside all of us still wants to know where to draw the line: how much does God want from me?

Old Testament law required God's people to give a tithe (tenth) of their income to the church.[209] Including charitable efforts, temple sacrifices, and other mandates, however, the total was as high as 25 percent.[210] The New Testament encourages giving without providing specific numbers, and reminds us that if we fail to give, we don't harm God, we only harm ourselves (and our church, since we're all part of the same body): "Whoever sows sparingly will also reap sparingly," Scripture says. "Whoever sows bountifully will also reap bountifully."[211] Since giving is a

---

209. Num. 18:21–29, 27:30.

210. Driscoll and Breshears, *Doctrine*, 393; cf. Deut. 12:10–11, 17–18, 14:22–29; Lev. 19:9–10; Neh. 10:32–33.

211. 2 Cor. 9:6.

matter of the heart, and since Jesus fulfilled the law, God's people are to give as a grateful response to his love, not to fulfill a pre-determined percentage or quota.

Contrary to what many popular preachers have taught, "bountifully" is not a promise of material gain. We sow to reap spiritual blessings on earth and tangible treasures in heaven. The more we give generously, the more we will store up treasure in heaven (see chapter 7), and the more we might see Jesus' mission progress in our lifetime.

We don't give to the church because God needs our money. He reminds us in Psalm 50, "If I were hungry, I would not tell you, for the world and its fullness are mine."[212] What he's truly after is us. It is impossible to love God and not give.[213] And without a hard-and-fast percentage that mandates how much we give, we're back to the biblical qualifiers for generous giving: cheerful, sacrificial, and regular. C.S. Lewis sums it up well:

> I am afraid the only safe rule is to give more than we can spare. In other words, if our expenditure on comforts, luxuries, amusements, etc., is up to the standard common among those with the same income as our own, we are probably giving away too little. If our charities do not at all pinch or hamper us, I should say they are too small. There ought to be things we should like to do and cannot do because our charities expenditure [giving] excludes them.[214]

212. Ps. 50:12.

213. Matt. 6:21, 24.

214. Lewis, *Mere Christianity*, 86.

If our giving does not require us to trust God, there's a good chance we're simply going through the motions. As a pastor, I often taught that giving 10 percent to your church is a good place to start. For most people, 10 percent represents an amount that challenges them to walk faithfully in this area of their life. Depending on the circumstances of life, for some a tenth isn't enough. For others it may be too much. Craig Blomberg speculates, "If most affluent Western Christians were to be honest about the extent of their surplus, they would give considerably higher than 10 percent." [215]

In any case, the absence of a specific mandate creates dependence on God because we must actively seek his will for our finances. We can't identify a percentage and then "set it and forget it." Giving is meant to be an ongoing, dynamic component of lives lived in worship of Jesus. When we understand the joy of giving in response to God's grace, "how much does God want" becomes "how much can I give?"

WHO GETS THE MONEY?

When I was a pastor, I told our congregation to direct their regular giving toward the church. Now that I'm just another average guy in the pews, I'd still say the same thing. As Christians, our generosity should most definitely extend beyond the church, but never exclude the church.

The church is not an organization. The church is a family. [216] Favoring some other charity or cause above

215. Blomberg, *Neither Poverty nor Riches*, 199.

216. Rom. 8:15–17; Eph. 2:19; 1 Tim. 5:1–2.

your church indicates either a misunderstanding of the biblical definition of church, or negligence. It would be like a father who works hard, earns a living, and then buys a bunch of new clothes for the kids down the street while his own children run around wearing garbage sacks. A Christian's first obligation in giving is to contribute to the health and well-being of the church. [217]

Exclusively cause-oriented giving could also represent a measure of pride ("proceeds from this shirt benefit my image"), and a lack of passion for the gospel. Causes come and go like fads—whether they're resolved or not, sadly. Only the message of Jesus' death and resurrection in our place offers consistent, universal, and eternal hope. God's chosen vehicle for this message is the church, so we have a responsibility to make sure she's healthy.

COMMON OBJECTIONS TO CHURCH GIVING

We can usually think up plenty of reasons not to steward our money well. Sometimes it's a matter of ignorance or immaturity, and we need someone to explain what the Bible says on the subject. Other times it's just an excuse, and we need correction. Here are some of the excuses I've encountered over the years, and my efforts to address them.

Money is a private matter between me and God.

There is nothing magical or especially holy about money. It's just a gift. A tool. We can wield it wisely or foolishly,

---

217. Gal. 6:10.

so within a healthy church we need to hold each other accountable for how we use it. Though we will give a personal account to God for how we steward our resources,[218] he has given us these resources in part to help build his kingdom and spread the gospel, which is not a solitary, private accomplishment, but work that is carried out by the church.[219]

Plus, given the amount of airtime and gravity money gets in Scripture, if we can talk about prayer, marriage, parenting, worship, and so on, then surely we can talk about this integral component of discipleship. That's not to say it will be easy. As I mentioned in the introduction, Americans consider credit card debt to be the greatest conversation taboo, more sensitive than love life, salary, weight, politics, or religion.[220]

I need to save money before I can give any.

Saving or spending should not replace giving. When the economy lags, our idols tend to shift from rash spending to incessant hoarding. Regardless of circumstances, God is trustworthy,[221] so we must avoid the extremes of over-consumption and excessive self-reliance.[222]

---

218. Matt. 25:14–30.

219. Acts 2:44–47; 2 Cor. 9:1–5.

220. Crouch, "Poll: Card debt the No. 1 taboo subject," CreditCards.com.

221. Ps. 73:23–26.

222. Matt. 6:28–33; Luke 13:21.

Churches are all about the money.
Jesus spoke about money more than any church I've ever attended. It's not about the money. It's about the heart, and the money is a helpful indicator of whether a church's heart is for Jesus or for self. In addition, if we truly believe in the mission of God expressed through his church, we should possess a desire to see that mission flourish with the help of our collective resources.

I don't trust the church.
Unfortunately, financial abuse at a few churches have damaged the reputation of all churches. I understand, and I would encourage you to talk to one of the leaders in the church in order to find out what sort of accountability is in place so that you can proceed to give in good conscience. That said, resist unwarranted and unfair suspicion. Blanket distrust of church in general may indicate another underlying issue worth further discussion and prayer.

We shouldn't talk about giving because the Bible says to give in secret.
Secrecy is a spiritual discipline that is appropriate under certain circumstances and with right motives,[223] but the Bible also includes many examples of public benevolence.[224] Jesus says, "Let your light shine before men, that they may see your good deeds and praise your Father in heaven."[225]

---

223. Matt. 6.4.

224. Mark 14:3–9; Luke 21:1–4; Acts 4:36–37.

225. Matt. 5:16.

Paul even encourages healthy competition when it comes to giving, [226] and givers in the early church publicly presented their offerings. [227] Again, the difference is the heart: what's your motive? If you want everybody to know about your giving, why? Do you want recognition, or do you want to encourage others? If you don't want anybody to know about your giving, why? Are you ashamed, or is there a legitimate reason why the details would be distracting?

I can't give—I'm a poor college student.

Our culture encourages college students to live beyond their means by taking out massive loans against an uncertain future. Debt in the form of financial aid is not wrong, but it's not something to be entered into without serious consideration and wise counsel. While investing in a career track and establishing discretionary spending habits, many college students practice little to no sacrifice. Start somewhere. Also, remember that stewardship includes time. Your church needs some time from the folks who can give more dollars, and some dollars from the folks who can give more time.

I can't give—I don't have anything.

"When people tell me they can't afford to tithe," says Randy Alcorn, "I ask them, 'If your income was reduced by 10 percent would you die?' They say, 'No.' And I say, 'Then

226. 2 Cor. 9:1–5.

227. Acts 4:35.

you've admitted that you can afford to tithe. It's just that you don't want to."[228]

Start simple, start small—start anywhere. God will grow your faith. If you never give God anything to work with, nothing will change. Give him room to cultivate in you a generous, faithful heart.

I want to give, but I just keep forgetting.

Invite others to hold you accountable. Pursue discipline. Set a calendar reminder on your computer or phone and give online.

Participation in the local church can't simply be a business exchange where we essentially pay for religious services or give to satisfy our conscience. Jesus calls us to be all in, but this will look different in various seasons of life. Some may have few dollars but lots of hours to volunteer. Others may be in a frantic season of work when all they have time to do is write a tithe check.

We can't impose unhealthy legalisms and quotas on the church body. Life circumstances are always changing, and the Bible gives no grounds for such mandates. At the same time, church members must not justify their lack of involvement with excuses. We need the wisdom and help of the Holy Spirit and church family to avoid sin and align our hearts with the work God has called us to do.

---

228. Alcorn, *The Treasure Principle*, 66.

Generosity beyond the church

A generous lifestyle does not stop with the church, like a checkbox on your Christian to-do list. Look for diverse and creative ways to be generous in your daily life. What organizations are doing good work in your community? How can you be generous in your workplace? Are there any families in your neighborhood experiencing hard times?

It's great to get in the habit of spontaneous generosity as well. Jesus celebrates many instances of spur-of-the-moment giving.[229] Here are some ways you could surprise and bless people with generosity this week:

- Tip large—double the price of your latte or meal.
- Buy dinner for the couple next to you, or the car behind you in the drive-thru.
- Bring your wife a surprise gift card.
- Take your kids out for ice cream.
- Buy donuts for your co-workers (or low-fat Greek yoghurt).
- If you're dining in the city, box up an extra meal and give it to a homeless person.
- Mow your neighbor's lawn.
- Read the newspaper for stories about local needs you could help meet.
- Offer free babysitting to young families in your church.
- Bring a meal or clean house for a family with a new baby.

---

229. Luke 10:30-37; John 12:1-8; Matt. 19:21.

The beautiful thing about generosity is that it often begets generosity. Live a generous life and watch a generous culture develop in your wake. This makes for good business, good family life, and I guarantee your friends will love spending time with you.

GOD SAVES STINGY SINNERS

When I was a new Christian, I didn't want to part with "my" hard-earned money. I was going to school and working at a restaurant, so giving money to the church didn't make a ton of sense. But since the Bible says it's important, I decided to give it a shot.

I was quite pleased with myself when I decided to drop $10 per week in the offering. The more I read the Bible, however, the more I realized that my contribution was merely a token gesture. For me, $10 in no way represented the sort of generous, sacrificial, worshipful giving that God had called me to.

Did he strike me down for my pride? Did he mock me for my ignorance? Hardly. As a loving Father, he sent the Holy Spirit to convict me of my sin and graciously and patiently encouraged me to give more and more, while at the same time building my faith in his continued provision and promises. No longer filthy rags offered with self-serving hands,[230] my gifts were becoming "a fragrant offering, a sacrifice acceptable and pleasing to God"[231] because they came from a heart redeemed by his Son.

---

230. Isa. 64:6.

231. Phil. 4:18.

We can never out-give our generous God.[232] This reality should always keep us in humble pursuit of his grace.

232. Ps. 16:11; Mal. 3:10; John 4:14.

CHAPTER NINE
MULTIPLY IT

*"Blessed are those servants whom the master
finds awake when he comes."*
—*Jesus* [233]

You will die.

Between today and that final day, what will you do with your money? Your time? Your energy? What sort of legacy will you leave when you go?

As we've discussed, the Parable of the Talents tells the story of three servants who receive a sum of money from their master. Two put the money to use, and it multiplied. In describing these events, Jesus commends these men with the words that all of us long to hear, "Well done, good and faithful servant. You have been faithful over a little; I will set you over much. Enter into the joy of your master."[234]

Godly stewardship doesn't aim for breaking even. Godly stewardship uses the gifts God has given to achieve an impact that extends beyond our own personal existence.

---

233. Luke 12:37.

234. Matt. 25:23.

DREAM BIG

John Piper says, "We waste our lives when we do not pray and think and dream and plan and work toward magnifying God in all spheres of life." [235] Where do you want to go? What are you pursuing? What drives you? What bugs you? What do you want to see changed—in your life, in your city, in the world?

For Christians, we've got the Holy Spirit working with us. Dream really big. "To be truly ambitious, our dreams need to reach into the next generation," says author Dave Harvey. "A biblical definition of success means we transfer the work to them, positioning them to run stronger and farther, while we cheer them on." [236] Legacy.

Though finances are a piece of this puzzle, your life amounts to more than the money in your bank account. Here are some questions to get you thinking about the various pieces of the puzzle and how they fit together in one big, long-term picture. Consider the answers you'd like to give ten, twenty-five, or fifty years from now, and on the last day of your life:

Walk with Jesus – Who will be impacted by my walk with Jesus? A particular age group, culture, neighbor, family member?

Giving – How much will I give between today and my last day? Have I given generously throughout my life, and will

---

235. John Piper, *Don't Waste Your Life* (Wheaton, IL: Crossway, 2003), 32.

236. Harvey, *Rescuing Ambition*, 200.

I continue to do so through my estate, if God has provided me with that kind of abundance?

Family – What will my family look like? How many children? Where will we live?

Friendships – Who will my friends be? To whom will I have been a friend?

Mission – What will I have done in obedience to Jesus' commandment to "make disciples of all nations" and fulfill the Great Commission?[237]

Career – What will I have spent my life working on or working for?

Housing – Will I pass on real estate as part of my legacy?[238]

Finances – What will I leave behind financially and to whom?[239] Where will the money God has entrusted to me have the greatest impact for the gospel?

The questions you ask today will ultimately shape the legacy you leave at the end of your life. In between, you'll need a plan.

---

237. Matt. 28:19.

238. Prov. 19:4.

239. Prov. 13:22.

PLAN BIG, BUT LET GOD BE GOD

I'm not sure who said it first, but I like it: The difference between a vision and an achievement is a plan. A plan takes our desired future and turns it into reasonable, specific steps we can take in succession to achieve our goals.

Proverbs says, "A man plans his course, but the LORD determines his steps."[240] We need to plan, we need to write things down, we need to pray for specific direction in our lives, but we also need to hold our plans in an open hand for God to chart our course. That's okay. He's God. He's allowed to do that. Your plan will change as he shapes your life and your convictions, but you still need to plan.

God is not Santa Clause. Our plans are not a wish list that we hand him in exchange for our good deeds. The purpose of a plan is good stewardship. We want to do our best to multiply the resources he has given us in order to make highest and best use of God's gifts. The legacy you leave summarizes your faithfulness and stewardship of everything God has entrusted to you for his glory and the good of others.

WHERE TO BEGIN

Maybe you've neglected to plan because you feel too young. Or too old. Or too busy. No matter your stage of life, however, as long as you have life, you have something

240. Prov. 16:9.

to steward, and a plan will help do so faithfully.

A great place to start is the budget we discussed in chapter 3. Here are a few more ways to grow in stewardship, develop a plan, and multiply the resources God has given you, as you move through various stages in life.

ADVICE FOR CHILDREN (VIA PARENTS)

Teach your kids about Jesus and their need for his grace. Generosity stems from Jesus. We may be excellent money managers, able to instruct our children in the way of financial planning, but if neither our children nor we understand the gospel, then all the planning in the world amounts to nothing.

Invite your kids into the conversation.

Too often we parents go about our day doing chores, paying bills, running errands, and planning for the future, all the while forgetting to invite our kids to participate. Through this experience, we can teach them things like responsibility, work ethic, joy, and decision-making.

Teach your kids to divide their money into three categories: give, save, and spend.

When your kids get money for birthdays, holidays, and allowance, help them plan what to do with it. I'll never forget when my son opened a fifth birthday card from his grandparents. There was some money in it, and he blurted out, "Yes! Now I can pay my bills!" He didn't have many bills as a five-year-old, but I loved the fact that he was beginning to think through stewardship.

Don't stifle innovation; allow failure.

I know it's a lot of work to set up the lemonade stand, but what a great opportunity to teach your kids about work, business principles, and managing finances. As your kids get ideas, take the time to encourage them and invest in them so that these mini-ventures can be used as teaching opportunities—whether or not they're financially profitable.

Engage your kids and teach them discernment.

Most parents expect their kids to learn through osmosis rather than intentional development. And the truth is, without any parental discernment to guide them, kids will absorb their life lessons, thanks to marketing, friends, the Internet—none of which tend to rely on the principles of Scripture for instruction. Kids need to be equipped to recognize the difference between truth and lies.

Model generosity.

Practice what you preach. Don't give to impress your children, but don't hide it from them either. When you miss the mark, confess your sin to your family and let your kids see that dad and mom need a Savior, too. Since generosity flows from grace, we can use it as a tool to teach about Jesus.

ADVICE FOR SINGLES

Establish giving patterns now.

I hate to say it, but single people can be incredibly selfish. We're all selfish, I get that. But young singles excel in this vice. I know from experience. You're in a season of your life in which you have a lot of time and probably excess money to manage. What you do now sets the course for the next twenty years. Think about what it would look like to set a pattern of giving and serving, one that chips away at selfishness rather than reinforces it.

Learn from others that are ahead of you.

If you're young, be sure to learn from mature, established adults further along in life. Ask them about their successes, their mistakes, what worked for them, and what they would do differently. I assure you they'll have a list.

Consider what you'd bring into a marriage.

Odds are, you'll get married some day. In the meantime, are you working on building up your shoe collection, or are your saving for a down payment on a house? There is a huge difference between debt and cash when it comes to starting a marriage. I've worked with couples beginning life together under a cloud of $100,000 in student loans and credit card debt. The burden can be smothering, and it often becomes the dominating issue for many, many years of the marriage. I've also worked with couples that brought savings into their marriage, and the financial freedom they enjoy is life-giving. What you do with your money in the present will have a profound impact on your marriage in the future. Start loving your future spouse now by practicing good stewardship.

Take advantage of compound interest when you're 18–30.
Rather than seizing the day by spending all your money as it comes in, seize the opportunity to multiply your money. Even if you never want to retire, someday you won't be able to work as hard or earn as much as you can when you're young. Invest enough so that you can continue to be generous in your old age, rather than hoarding your nest egg for yourself.

When you're young, the magic of compound interest is on your side. If you save $300 per month from ages 22–28 at an interest rate of 10 percent per year, your seven years' worth of savings will grow to $1 million by age sixty-five. If you start investing your $300 a month at age thirty-one, however, it'll take thirty-four years of saving to reach $1 million by sixty-five.[241] A 10 percent return may be optimistic, but the same principle applies: The younger you are, the more your savings is likely to grow. Even if you can only contribute a small amount, it's to your advantage to start right away. Be proactive.

Have fun.
Working toward goals, plans, and a vision for your future doesn't mean you can't enjoy God's blessings, gifts, and

---

241. Erin Burt, "Behold the Miracle of Compounding," Kiplinger, November 8, 2007 (updated in 2011), http://www.kiplinger.com/article/saving/T063-C006-S001-behold-the-miracle-of-compounding.html.

grace to you today. If your priorities are in order, it's both/and, not either/or. Remember, preparing for the future should look and feel much different than banking on the future [242] or worrying about the future. [243]

ADVICE FOR MARRIED COUPLES

No secrets.

Plan together. Financial secrecy destroys marriages. It usually starts small but anything kept in the dark will grow into a massive shadow that will cloud and destroy the oneness God intends for marriage. If you are not 100 percent honest with your spouse about your debt, spending habits, secret hobbies, and such, put this book down immediately and begin the confession and repentance process. Jesus died for your sin, and he will forgive you. If your spouse loves Jesus, he or she probably will forgive you, too.

Leverage each other's strengths.

Hopefully, one of you is more administratively gifted than the other, so that person will be better at balancing the checking account and managing the spreadsheets. Use those gifts effectively.

Too often one spouse leaves the financial management completely up to the other. Both husband and wife need to have their heads in the game: know the budget,

242. Luke 12:19–20.

243. Luke 12:22–23.

know your giving, and know where you stand financially as a family. If possible, make the experience fun. Talk numbers over ice cream and make a date out of it.

Understand each other's weaknesses.

Financial conflict and stress lead to way more divorces than they should; money is the number one thing American couples fight about.[244] I've found that savers often marry spenders, which isn't wrong, but the dichotomy can lead to all kinds of marital strife if you don't understand one another. Don't point fingers. Start by knowing and owning your own style and sin patterns (saver, spender, cheapskate, frivolous, coveter) so that you can learn to communicate humbly and effectively with your spouse and build a united plan that honors God together.

Use money as a gift to foster oneness.

We've talked a lot about giving in this book—how about giving to your spouse? Do you have a fund in your budget dedicated to loving your spouse, or enough margin that allows you to spontaneously bless them? When your wife is stressed, send her to get a pedicure. When your husband needs a gift, figure out a way to make it happen. Stress tends to dominate our financial lives, and we forget to have fun. This is yet another way we fall into devoting ourselves to money as a god, allowing it to affect our moods, our mental health, or our marriages rather than receiving it as a gift from God. Figure out how to use

244. Dave Ramsey, *Financial Peace Revisited* (New York: Viking, 2003), 195.

money to have fun in your marriage, which will foster love and intimacy.

Live on one income.
At some point in your life, either by choice or by necessity, your family will need to survive on one income. If you can organize your budget and accomplish this ahead of time, you'll be much better prepared when the crisis, the cutbacks, or the babies arrive. A second income that you don't "need" provides an amazing opportunity to be generous, save up, or pay off debt, all of which will give you a firmer foundation for your future. Too often newly married couples immediately adjust their spending to match the double income, and they begin to live a lifestyle that isn't sustainable.

On a similar note, be sure to include life insurance in your plan in the event that one spouse dies and the other is left with a mortgage, student loans, young children, or other financial obligations. Make this arrangement sooner rather than later, because premiums are much cheaper when you're young.

ADVICE FOR MIDDLE AGE AND OLDER
Don't defer or compartmentalize ministry.
Many successful Christian business people wrestle with whether they should trade their secular vocation for a life of full-time "ministry" serving the church. This may be God's call on your life, but I would have a few pastoral questions to ask before you quit your day job:

- *Do you believe that, by virtue of being a Christian, you are already in full-time ministry?* Every Christian is an ambassador of Jesus, no matter if their work is "secular" or "spiritual." Just because it's not your job doesn't mean you still can't serve people, share the gospel, pray, and be a missionary to your neighborhood, culture, and spheres of influence.

- *Are you being faithful where you are?* Many people think switching to a more ministry-oriented career will provide the spiritual juice and accountability that seem to be lacking. Oftentimes, however, changing circumstances is simply a way to avoid dealing with sin. The problem usually resides in our hearts, not our circumstances. If that's the case, don't go anywhere. Start repenting and see what God does. If you are being faithful where you're at and feel called to something else, be free in Christ to explore where the Holy Spirit might be leading.

- *Did you know that giving is a spiritual gift?*[245] It may feel more holy to drop everything you're doing to volunteer full-time at your church or move to a developing country, but if God has blessed you with great business skills and financial success, your role in the kingdom of God may be to make a ton of money and give a ton away.

---

245. Rom. 12:8.

Share your story, your wisdom, your success, and your failures.

When it comes to life stages, I have the least amount of experience in the middle and old age categories, so I invited some seasoned friends to share their thoughts: [246]

> *Instead of "grabbing all you can get and enjoying it now," we should practice intentional living that points to eternity as our source of joy, peace, and contentment. It could be that God allows you more discretionary time and resources as your earthly clock ticks down, and how you choose to invest those reflects what is most treasured in your heart. My dad used to say, "You win or lose by the way you choose." We should make certain we choose wisely in this area, as the stakes are very high to future generations.*
> —Dave, age 50

> *The vision I had of retirement led me to follow a steady course for many years. The path included established goals to work hard, sacrifice, spend wisely, save diligently, practice delayed gratification, give faithfully, and to be content with what we had. My success in these areas varied significantly, but by God's grace, the original vision was realized.*
>
> *My vision for retirement was not very different from the same lifestyle and goals I used to get there. The main difference was trading "production" for "time." I wanted to have a life where people, grandbabies,*

---

246. Names have been changed.

relationships, and service didn't have to compete with my production—the need for income, a full-time job, and all the accompanying trappings.

I understand the value of work, and that production and time can co-exist, but I also know myself and my tendencies well enough that, for me, retirement had a better chance to succeed than a longer or scaled-back career.

This all sounds fine in theory, but will be wasted if my life does not bring glory to God. I am praying that God's grace will continue to lead me, that I continue to grow closer to him, and that my life brings him glory and blessing to others.

—Stan, age 60

Most of us grew up with the thought that retirement is what Grandpa did when he didn't have to go to work anymore and was able to spend more time with us kids. And to be certain, retirement is some of that. But retirement as it relates to our vocation is much different than what we do with our lives after our primary vocational responsibilities have ended. We never retire from our faith. Christians never retire from serving Jesus and community. We are called to serve and the only change is the address of where we work.

—John, age 55

To older men and women: your war stories are invaluable. Share them with the young people in your church and community. Take young folks out for coffee.

Enjoy the privilege of multiplying the work of the gospel beyond your life and into the life of others. It's never too early or too late to start thinking about how your time and money can pave the way for future generations.

BETTER TOGETHER

What would it look like if everyone in your church used their resources to serve one common mission? What would it look like if other churches joined? What would it look like if we as individuals stopped worshiping money as a god, and received it as a gift—a useful tool in the kingdom of the true God?

We could see thousands of churches planted in our lifetime, and hundreds of thousands of people meet Jesus as a result. Our faithful stewardship could bless generations to come, and our children's children's children's children could hear the gospel as a result of how we live today.

That is my prayer for all of us stewards in Jesus' kingdom. The best way to multiply the impact of our money is by investing it together for God's glory. The church is a body, and we won't get very far as a leg, an eyeball, or a finger out on our own. "If all were a single member, where would the body be?," Paul asks. "As it is, there are many parts, yet one body."[247]

From our good, faithful, and loving God we've received forgiveness, salvation, Jesus, the Holy Spirit, a church family, the kingdom, life, and the message of the

247. 1 Cor. 12:19–20.

gospel to share with the world. We have every reason to be grateful, love one another, and work together to use our gifts to the glory of Jesus, for the good of others, and for the joy of being what we were created to be. "Thanks be to God for his inexpressible gift!"[248]

---

248. 2 Cor. 9:15.

CHAPTER TEN
DON'T WORRY ABOUT IT

"Keep your life free from love of money, and
be content with what you have, for he has said,
'I will never leave you nor forsake you.'"
—Hebrews 13:5

Money is a good, necessary, extremely helpful gift from God. It is also an enticing, destructive, and terrible god. I sincerely pray that this book has helped you put money in its rightful place as an instrument to glorify Jesus, a gauge to assess the spiritual health of your heart, and a blessing from God that's perfectly fine to enjoy.

NEXT STEPS

The lessons, ideas, and principles I've included throughout this book require some specific practical application if they're going to do you any good. Here's a basic punch list of priorities to get started: [249]

1. Give
2. Purchase life insurance
3. Budget (see appendix for sample template)
4. Create an emergency fund

---

249. For additional advice, templates, techniques, and tips, check out some of the books I've recommended in the appendix.

5. Pay off debt
6. Save for retirement
7. Save for large purchase (house, college)
8. Estate planning (will, legacy giving)
9. Breathe and enjoy life

Always begin with give. After that, the order will vary depending on your priorities. As you get to work defining the specifics of your plan, your money, and your life, remember to pace yourself.

Keep it simple.
People often make financial planning more complicated than it needs to be. You don't need expensive software, a CPA degree, online banking, or lots of mutual funds to be a good steward. Find a system that works for you. The simpler it is, the easier it will be to stick to it.

Stay on track.
As you begin to give and sacrifice, you'll feel the pinch. Temptation will creep in and the path of least resistance will start to look pretty good. Don't give in. Know that you will be tempted and prepare accordingly. Memorize Scripture, seek accountability, and pray a lot.

Don't go it alone.
Proverbs says, "Without counsel plans fail, but with many advisers they succeed."[250] Ask for wisdom and

250. Prov. 15:22.

accountability from trusted advisers: friends, small group, family. Listen to what they have to say, even if it hurts. [251] Also, husbands and wives must work together to steward their resources as one.

You're not in heaven.

The world is broken and life rarely fits together like a nice puzzle. Don't spend a ton of energy trying to create heaven on earth. Creation is subject to frustration, [252] and you will get very, very frustrated if you try to make things perfect. Don't replace money with good stewardship as your god. Work with what you've got, and worship Jesus.

Carry your own load; share your burdens.

Galatians 6 says, "Bear one another's burdens," but also, "Each will have to bear his own load." [253] Your "load" refers to your responsibility: your budget, your money, your giving. Don't make somebody take care of what you should be taking care of. At the same time, when a legitimate burden arises (death, job loss, illness, tragedy), don't be too proud to ask for help. God gave us a large family (the church) in part so that we can make sure everyone is cared for.

Stewardship is a lifestyle.

Managing your money and your resources well takes more than reading a book or completing a study course. Like all

---

251. Prov. 9:8.

252. Rom. 8:20.

253. Gal. 6:2, 5.

aspects of discipleship, being a good steward takes a life of faith and repentance, love and obedience. We need ongoing teaching, prayer, and time with Jesus to continually ask the question, "How can I be most faithful with what I've been given?"

Take it one day at a time.
It's important to think long-term, but don't get overwhelmed by the fifty-year big vision. "Tomorrow will worry about itself," Jesus said.[254] Ask God for wisdom each day, and begin there, starting with today.

If you only remember one thing . . .
Over and over again, throughout Scripture, God assures us that we can trust him,[255] because he is a good God.[256] *Don't worry!*

"Do not be anxious," Jesus tells us in Luke 12. "But if God so clothes the grass, which is alive in the field today, and tomorrow is thrown into the oven, how much more will he clothe you, O you of little faith! And do not seek what you are to eat and what you are to drink, nor be worried."[257]

But we do get anxious, especially when it comes to money. No matter what we say about God with our mouths, as long as worry resides in our hearts we do not believe him. Rather than justify this anxiety, confess the

254. Matt. 6:34, NIV.

255. Matt. 6; Luke 12:24, 30, 32; Phil. 4:6; 1 Pet. 5.

256. Luke 11:13, John 10:10–11.

257. Luke 12:22, 28–29.

truth. God is not surprised. As with any sin, freedom from worry requires admission of guilt. Confession is a humble declaration, such as:

I have committed treason against the kingdom of God by placing my hope and trust in an earthly kingdom of money and stuff. I need Jesus' death in my place, and I need the power of the Holy Spirit in order to change. Thank you Father, for your grace.

Our worries reveal our slavery to sin. Our inability to cease worrying reveals our helplessness. Our helplessness reveals our need for God's grace. God's grace sets us free from worry and enables us to change through repentance. Practically speaking, financial repentance includes the proper planning we've discussed throughout the book. To illustrate, here's how such planning can serve to calm certain concerns:

Common Worry	Stewardship Plan
Unemployment	Maintain a savings account to cover living expenses for three months.
Sudden crisis	Build an emergency fund for unplanned expenses.
Spouse's death	Purchase enough life insurance to pay off all debt and provide for ongoing living expenses.
Can't afford kids	Begin living off of one income; research cost of children; budget accordingly.

Common Worry	Stewardship Plan
Retirement	Use a retirement calculator to plan ahead; adjust lifestyle as necessary.

Insofar as it's possible, good stewards prepare for the realities of life. Stuff happens. Don't dwell on the possibilities; trust God and plan accordingly. "Do not be anxious" does not mean, "Be lazy and make no plans." Wishful thinking is just optimistic worry. Instead, work hard and make a plan. Fight worry by acknowledging it and then chart a way forward.

On the flipside, prudent planning may still mask a sinful heart. A good plan may address our symptoms, but only true repentance can deal with the root cause of those symptoms which proceed from our heart. If you worry a lot about your spouse dying, for example, purchasing a life insurance policy may alleviate financial concerns, but anxiety will remain because savings accounts and insurance policies cannot provide ultimate security.

Jesus is not Bob Marley. Granted, it is hard to worry while listening to reggae. But when Jesus says "don't worry," it's not an empty encouragement that just makes us feel better for a moment. Jesus helps us. And he invites us to something greater that eclipses our material concerns. "Seek his kingdom, and these things will be added to you."[258] This isn't a distraction technique. It's not, *Stay busy enough and you'll forget to worry!* Nor is it, *Don't*

---

258. Luke 12:31.

worry about money because material things aren't important. It's a promise: Don't worry about "what you are to eat and what you are to drink"[259] because God will provide what you need. Seek the kingdom of God, and you will be satisfied.

Jesus doesn't belittle our material concerns. He promises that God will provide for them, which means we can spend our time and energy participating in a cause greater than our own survival. Our job is to seek the kingdom; his job is to take care of us along the way, according to his will.

I struggle with this regularly. I forget God's relentless faithfulness to meet every one of my needs, and I revert to the mindset that I'm the one in charge. I'm not. He's got it. This perspective is more powerful than circumstances. It's an attitude that changes everything.

Joy does not come from abundance.

Sorrow does not come from poverty.

"Keep your life free from love of money, and be content with what you have, for he has said, 'I will never leave you nor forsake you.'"[260]

IN CLOSING

However much is in your bank account at the moment, make the most of what you have. Don't get complacent and play it safe, but don't envy. Be content. And be thankful.

---

259. Luke 12:29.

260. Heb. 13:5.

Hopefully, you'll close this book with a lot to think about and a few things to do, but remember that life isn't a checklist. Don't let anxiety and guilt steal your smile. Money is a gift, but life is, too, and a far more precious one. Go live it.

Behold, what I have seen to be good and fitting is to eat and drink and find enjoyment in all the toil with which one toils under the sun the few days of his life that God has given him, for this is his lot. Everyone also to whom God has given wealth and possessions and power to enjoy them, and to accept his lot and rejoice in his toil—this is the gift of God. For he will not much remember the days of his life because God keeps him occupied with joy in his heart.

—Ecclesiastes 5:18–20

APPENDIX A

STUDY GUIDE

The following guide is for churches and small groups that want to dig into Money: God or Gift *together. Use this five-week curriculum as is, or adapt it, revise it, and hack it to suit your context.*

The Bible is chock-full of rich passages about finances, but Luke 12 touches on all of the big ideas in Money, *so I've chosen excerpts from that chapter as the Scriptural basis for each week's conversation.*

WEEK ONE

<u>Chapter 1: Hate it</u>

Relate together:
Did you get an allowance as a kid? What did you have to do to earn it, if anything?

Read together:
Luke 12:4–7 – "I tell you, my friends, do not fear those who kill the body, and after that have nothing more that they can do. But I will warn you whom to fear: fear him who, after he has killed, has authority to cast into hell. Yes, I tell you, fear him! Are not five sparrows sold for two pennies? And not one of them is forgotten before God. Why, even the hairs of your head are all numbered. Fear not; you are of more value than many sparrows."

Discuss together:
1. What worries nag you throughout the day and keep you up at night? What scares you? What does your anxiety reveal about your perception of God's character?
2. What does it mean to "fear" God? Why does Jesus use this language to describe an appropriate relationship with God, and how does love fit into the equation?
3. Do you have any expectations or goals for this study specifically related to your personal finance? Why are you here, and what do you hope to see as a result?

Pray together:
Ask the Holy Spirit to aid and bless your study with wisdom, conviction, encouragement, and change. Confess your fears and ask the Holy Spirit to lead you in repentance. Praise God for his forgiveness, love, and provision.

WEEK TWO

<u>Chapters 2–3: Steward it and budget it</u>

Relate together:
Your house is burning down. Everyone is safe and you can salvage one material possession, large or small. What do you keep?

Read together:
Luke 12:42–48 – And the Lord said, "Who then is the faithful and wise manager, whom his master will set over his household, to give them their portion of food at the proper time? Blessed is that servant whom his master will find so doing when he comes. Truly, I say to you, he will set him over all his possessions. But if that servant says to himself, 'My master is delayed in coming,' and begins to beat the male and female servants, and to eat and drink and get drunk, the master of that servant will come on a day when he does not expect him and at an hour he does not know, and will cut him in pieces and put him with the unfaithful. And that servant who knew his master's will but did not get ready or act according to his will, will receive a severe beating. But the one who did not know, and did what deserved a beating, will receive a light beating. Everyone to whom much was given, of him much will be required, and from him to whom they entrusted much, they will demand the more."

Discuss together:

1. Review the table on page 12. Look at the left-hand column and discuss the places where you are prone to greed instead of gratitude. Cultivate a thankful heart by sharing examples of God's goodness in your life, in your church, and in the promises of Scripture.

2. Are you more inclined to live according to prosperity theology or poverty theology? How does Jesus upend both of these errors?

3. What steps will you take this week in order to exercise better stewardship? (Ideas: create a budget; update the budget you already have; start a savings account.) Why does this matter?

Pray together:

Thank God for all of the good things he has entrusted to you. Ask for the Holy Spirit's help in stewarding these gifts well. Confess your grumbling, and praise God for his patience and grace that gives us hope for change.

WEEK THREE

<u>Chapters 4–6: Make it, spend it, and save it</u>

Relate together:
Talk about something you saved for over a long period of
time. What was the result? Was it worth it?

Read together:
Luke 12:15–21 – And he said to them, "Take care, and be on
your guard against all covetousness, for one's life does not
consist in the abundance of his possessions." And he told
them a parable, saying, "The land of a rich man produced
plentifully, and he thought to himself, 'What shall I do,
for I have nowhere to store my crops?' And he said, 'I will
do this: I will tear down my barns and build larger ones,
and there I will store all my grain and my goods. And I
will say to my soul, "Soul, you have ample goods laid up
for many years; relax, eat, drink, be merry."' But God said
to him, 'Fool! This night your soul is required of you, and
the things you have prepared, whose will they be?' So is
the one who lays up treasure for himself and is not rich
toward God."

Discuss together:
  1. When it comes to money, are you a spender or a saver?
     Explain your perspective to the group and invite
     feedback, especially from those who fall into the
     opposite camp.

2. What compels you to save, spend, or make more money? What fears drive you, in addition to any noble motives?

3. If an outsider were to observe your financial life for a week—how you make, spend, save, give, and otherwise use your money—what would they learn about your priorities? Ask your spouse or a close friend to give their honest assessment.

Pray together:

Praise God as the giver and sustainer of life. Confess the ways in which you've relied on money over God—for self worth, piece of mind, acceptance, or glory. Ask the Holy Spirit for his wisdom and active guidance as you go about making, spending, and saving the money God has entrusted to you.

WEEK FOUR

Chapters 7–8: Invest it and give it

Relate together:
What is one of the best material gifts you've ever received?

Read together:
Luke 12:32–34 – "Fear not, little flock, for it is your Father's good pleasure to give you the kingdom. Sell your possessions, and give to the needy. Provide yourselves with moneybags that do not grow old, with a treasure in the heavens that does not fail, where no thief approaches and no moth destroys. For where your treasure is, there will your heart be also."

Discuss together:
1. Randy Alcorn writes: "He who lays up treasures on earth spends his life backing away from his treasures. To him, death is loss. He who lays up treasures in heaven looks forward to eternity; he's moving daily toward his treasure. To him, death is gain."[261] Are you drifting toward your treasure or away from it? How can you tell?
2. Which aspect of biblical giving is most difficult for you: cheerful, sacrificial, or regular? What does repentance look like for you? Why are all three of these characteristics important?

---

261. Alcorn, *The Treasure Principle*, 45.

3. What random act of generosity will you try this week? (see page 89 for ideas)

Pray together:
Praise God for all of his generous gifts—name as many as time allows. Thank God for all of his generous gifts to come in heaven. Ask the Holy Spirit to help you recognize opportunities to extend generosity in your daily life.

WEEK FIVE

<u>Chapters 9–10: Multiply it and don't worry about it</u>

Relate together:

After you die, what is one word you hope people might use to describe you in remembrance?

Read together:

Luke 12:22–31 – And he said to his disciples, "Therefore I tell you, do not be anxious about your life, what you will eat, nor about your body, what you will put on. For life is more than food, and the body more than clothing. Consider the ravens: they neither sow nor reap, they have neither storehouse nor barn, and yet God feeds them. Of how much more value are you than the birds! And which of you by being anxious can add a single hour to his span of life? If then you are not able to do as small a thing as that, why are you anxious about the rest? Consider the lilies, how they grow: they neither toil nor spin, yet I tell you, even Solomon in all his glory was not arrayed like one of these. But if God so clothes the grass, which is alive in the field today, and tomorrow is thrown into the oven, how much more will he clothe you, O you of little faith! And do not seek what you are to eat and what you are to drink, nor be worried. For all the nations of the world seek after these things, and your Father knows that you need them. Instead, seek his kingdom, and these things will be added to you."

Discuss together:

1. Share some of your long-term goals. How has Jesus changed or shaped these plans?

2. Review the life stage advice on pages 97–106. Based on your season of life, which piece of counsel is most encouraging? Most challenging? How do you hope to change in light of this guidance?

3. What will you remember from this study and how do you hope it affects your life?

Pray together:

Surrender your goals, aspirations, and legacy to God. Pray for favor, guidance, and wisdom in these endeavors. Ask the Holy Spirit for the faith necessary to trust God with the outcome.

APPENDIX B

RECOMMENDED RESOURCES

BOOKS

Money, Possession, and Eternity
By Randy Alcorn
Alcorn's definitive book on the subject of stewardship expands on the same themes as *The Treasure Principle*.

The Treasure Principle: Unlocking the Secret of Joyful Giving
By Randy Alcorn
A very brief but excellent intro to biblical stewardship.

Neither Poverty nor Riches: A Biblical Theology of Possessions
By Craig Blomberg
A guided tour through the entire Bible using the lens of money and stewardship.

Doctrine: What Christians Should Believe
By Mark Driscoll and Gerry Breshears
The chapter "Stewardship: God Gives" explains stewardship within the context of the whole Bible.

Every Good Endeavor:
Connecting Your Work to God's Work
By Timothy Keller
A readable, comprehensive overview of the Bible's perspective on the purpose and value of work.

Desiring God: Meditations of a Christian Hedonist
By John Piper
Piper dedicates one chapter to money specifically, but the entire book provides helpful insight on what it means to make God our greatest treasure.

Don't Waste Your Life
By John Piper
How Christian stewardship is to be reflected in our lifestyle, our priorities, and what we treasure.

Financial Peace
By Dave Ramsey
Ramsey's first book takes a more general approach ("what to do") than *Total Money Makeover* ("how to do it").

Total Money Makeover
By Dave Ramsey
Practical financial advice that aligns with many of the principles found in Scripture.

Passing the Plate:
Why American Christians Don't Give More Money
By Christian Smith, Michael Emerson, Patricia Snell
A team of researchers present a landmark study on giving, Christians, and the church.

Running Scared: Fear, Worry, and the God of Rest
By Edward T. Welch
Great insight on a subject that drives our money decisions. Welch devotes a chapter to financial worry specifically.

Contagious Generosity:
Creating a Culture of Giving in Your Church
By Chris Willard and Jim Sheppard
Many pastors don't know how to broach the subject of money with their church. This book provides great perspective and practical ideas on the subject.

TOOLS

Mint.com
One of the first and still one of the best financial planning tools of the digital age. Mint is a totally free service that integrates all of your accounts in one place. The user-friendly interface allows you to budget, set goals, and track spending from your computer or phone.

Crown Financial
A money-related ministry that offers numerous training materials, calculators, and other financial planning tools online at crown.org.

Financial Peace University
One of many personal finance education courses established by Dave Ramsey and available at DaveRamsey.com.

BreadVault.com
For families with kids, BreadVault is a free app/online service that integrates financial education with technology, kind of like a virtual piggybank that allows you to save, invest, and give as a family.

Moonjar
For families that prefer old fashioned cash and coins over pixels, Moonjar is a moneybox for kids with three separate sections for saving, spending, and sharing. More info at moonjar.com

APPENDIX C

BUDGET TEMPLATE

There are many great budgeting tools available, but here is a basic template to help you get started. Look up Dave Ramsey or Crown Financial for further financial guidance.

	Monthly	Yearly	Notes
EARN			*Use net income (after taxes and deductions)*
Gross Wages			
Taxes/Deductions			
Retirement Deduction			
Other Income			*If "Other" income is taxable, be sure to save enough of your earnings to pay the IRS*
Total Income			
GIVE			
Church			*10% of earnings (suggested starting line)*
Other			
Total Giving			
DEBT			*List Mortgage in "Housing" (below)*
Student Loan			
Auto Loan			
Credit Card #1			
Credit Card #2			
Other			
Total Debt			*Make it a priority to pay off debt ASAP*
SAVE			
Emergency			
Retirement			
Other			*College, down payment, etc.*
Total Savings			

	Monthly	Yearly	Notes
SPEND			
Insurance			*Calculate how much you need to save per month*
Life			*Essential for sole providers*
Auto			
Home			
Housing			*Probably 0–40% of income*
Utilities			*Budget according to high-use months*
Electricity			
Water			
Trash			
Gas			
Auto			
Fuel			
Maintenance			
Groceries			*Probably 10%-30% of income*
Clothing			
Upkeep			*Replacing, fixing and cleaning things around the house*
Hygiene			*Toiletries, haircuts, etc.*
Recreation			
Eating Out			
Entertainment			
Hospitality			*Plan to bless others*
Mobile Phone			
Internet/TV/Phone			
Christmas			*Save a little each month to have money for gifts, dates, etc.*
Other			*Subscriptions, memberships— don't leave anything out*
Total Expenses			
TOTAL MARGIN			*This number should be close to zero (not negative). A good budget accounts for the majority of income and expenses*

ACKNOWLEDGEMENTS

Thank you to Jesus for your "grace upon grace" (John 1:16), including my wife (Crystal) and our four kiddos (Caleb, Kara, Orin, and Haley) who top the list of blessings you've graced me with.

Thank you to Andrew Myers. Without your faithful help, this book wouldn't exist.

ABOUT THE AUTHOR

Jamie Munson is a Montana native living in Seattle, Washington, where he has worked as a pastor, the co-president of a premium coffee company, and a consultant helping churches and businesses make the most of their God-given resources. Jamie and his wife, Crystal, have four kids, and together they enjoy sports, walks, family nights, marbles, traveling, and good laughs.

For speaking requests, consulting inquiries, and more leadership content, please visit jamiemunson.com.